# PARTICLE THEORIES:

*International Pâte de Verre and Other Cast Glass Granulations*

Susanne K. Frantz

with historical introductory essay by Jean-Luc Olivié

Museum of American Glass at Wheaton Village, Millville, New Jersey

A Special Exhibition
Museum of American Glass
at Wheaton Village

April 1, 2005 through December 31, 2005

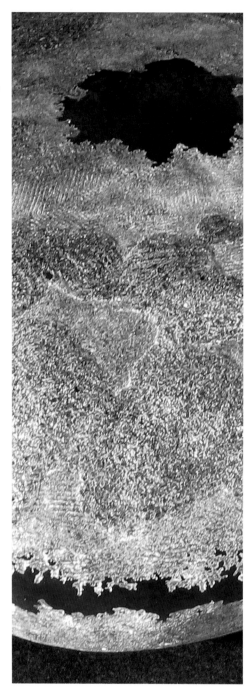

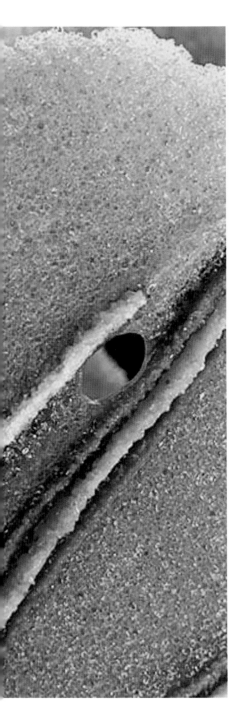

*Because the technique has several variations and ways of being finished, pâte de verre may be as light and thin as eggshell or as massive and dense as rock; it may appear pliable and waxy, or crystalline, like hoarfrost; textures may be porous and gritty, or smooth and shining; color detail is placed with precision or allowed to freely striate the inside and outside of the form.*

**Front and Back Cover (with detail)**

Penny Fuller (b. 1969)
Australia
Two *Leaf Vessels* from the *Autumn Series*, 2004
*Pâte de verre* (pastes of frit)
Orange Leaf: 1 3/4" x 7 3/4" x 4 3/4"
Yellow Leaf: 2" x 8" x 4 1/2"
Photo: G. Hancock

*CHECKLIST*

Dimensions are in inches: height x width x depth. The technical citations do not attempt to describe the complete process used to fabricate each piece. All objects, unless otherwise noted, are made in the basic *pâte de verre* methods or a variation and usually finished with one or more coldworking techniques. When known, additional details of interest are in parentheses.

For the purposes of this exhibition, basic *pâte de verre* is broadly defined as: premade glass reduced to a particalized consistency, placed in a refractory mold, fired in a kiln until fused or melted, cooled, and then freed from the mold.

copyright © 2005
ISBN 0-9742107-3-0 (HB)
ISBN 0-9742107-4-9 (PB)

Photography unless otherwise noted: The Lens Group
Corning Museum of Glass photographs: Nicholas Williams

Design: Libby Woolever, Chestertown, Maryland

Printing: Tri-Tech Canada, Toronto, Canada

This catalog was made possible by a generous grant
from the Davenport Family Foundation.

Wheaton Village strives to make exhibits, events and programs accessible to all visitors. Funding has been made possible in part by the New Jersey State Council on the Arts/Department of State, a Partner Agency of the National Endowment for the Arts, and the Geraldine R. Dodge Foundation. Wheaton Village received a general operating support grant from the New Jersey Historical Commission, a division of Cultural Affairs in the Department of State.

# Acknowledgments

The Museum of American Glass and Susanne K. Frantz would like to express their gratitude to all the artists who loaned their work and participated in the exhibition. We are also grateful to Paul Bombeke for his translation of Jean-Luc Olivié's essay.

We would also like to thank the following:

## Institutional lenders to the exhibition:

The Corning Museum of Glass, Corning, New York: Donna Ayers, Warren Bunn, Jill Thomas-Clark, Andrew Fortune, Lekova Giadam, Brandy Harold, Steven Hazlett, Stephen Koob, Joseph Maio, Tina Oldknow, David Whitehouse and Nicholas Williams; Rakow Research Library: Gail Bardhan

The Chrysler Museum, Norfolk, Virginia: Gary Baker and Sara Beth Walsh

Barry Friedman. Ltd., New York, New York: Barry Friedman and Carole Hochman

Bullseye Connection Gallery, Portland, Oregon: Lani McGregor

Elizabeth Leach Gallery, Portland, Oregon

Habatat Galleries, Royal Oak, Michigan: Ferdinand Hampson

Heller Gallery, New York, New York

Nancy Hoffman Gallery, New York, New York

Imago Galleries, Palm Desert, California

Leo Kaplan Modern, New York, New York

Liuli Gongfang Crystal Co., Ltd., Shanghai, China

Marx-Saunders Gallery, Chicago, Illinois

Tittot Ltd., Peitou, Taiwan: Yung-shan Wang and Jennifer Hsu

Susanne K. Frantz also extends her thanks to Susan Gogan, President of Wheaton Village and the Wheaton Village Board of Trustees, the Museum of American Glass, and especially Gay LeCleire Taylor, Elizabeth Wilk, Pat Hemsley, and Dianne Wood. And to these patient individuals who generously extended their support and shared their expertise:

| | | |
|---|---|---|
| Rebecca Africano | Melanie Hunter | Jennifer Opie |
| Anna Boothe | Antoine Leperlier | Kirstie Rea |
| Dagmar Brendstrup | Marianne Maderna | Mayumi (Shino) Shinohara |
| Grace Cochrane | Audrey Mann | Elizabeth Swinburne |
| Keith Cummings | Jack Martin | Angela Thwaites |
| Fritz Dreisbach | Elizabeth McClure | Karla Trinkley and Will Dexter |
| Kate Elliott | Yoriko Mizuta | Sylvie Vandenhoucke |
| Diana Hobson | Jean-Luc Olivié | Harumi Yukatake |

## Exhibition Sponsors

Accor Hotel

Air France

Art Alliance for Contemporary Glass

The Davenport Family Foundation

and with support from the British Council

# Foreword

Over the past thirty years, the Museum of American Glass at Wheaton Village has organized numerous exhibits exploring different facets of glass made in the United States. This year marks a turning point in the Museum's ambitious exhibition schedule. This exhibit, "Particle Theories: International *Pâte de Verre* and Other Cast Glass Granulations," is the first time the Museum has presented a show focused on a specific technique of glass making created by international artists.

Although, *pâte de verre* (paste of glass or glass paste) probably dates back to ancient times, it was revived in France in the late 19th century. Interest in the technique waned by the early 20th century. The process was again revived in the late 1970s and continues to intrigue artists today.

When Susanne K. Frantz, former Curator of 20th-Century Glass at The Corning Museum of Glass, agreed to become our guest curator, lengthy discussions ensued. We concurred that no exhibition on *pâte de verre* would be complete without opening the show to international artists. Also, we agreed on the importance of telling the history of *pâte de verre* by including late 19th- and early 20th-century French examples. Jean-Luc Olivié, Curator of Glass at the Musée des Arts Décoratifs, the Louvre, Paris, and one of the world's foremost authorities on the history of *pâte de verre*, accepted the task of writing the introductory essay for this catalog.

The Museum of American Glass is pleased to present this exhibition curated by Susanne K. Frantz. With her expertise, the fascinating and difficult subject of *pâte de verre* is, for the first time, fully explored.

**Gay LeCleire Taylor**
*Director/Curator*
Museum of American Glass

# The Mythologies, Origins, and Developments of *Pâte de Verre*

by Jean-Luc Olivié,
Curator, Centre du Verre, Musée des Arts Décoratifs, Paris

Sculptor Henry Cros (1840-1907) did not consider what he named *pâte de verre* to be a technical invention; instead, Cros thought of it as the "restitution of a principle completely forgotten today." Introduced by Cros in the 1880s, *pâte de verre* appeared within the context of historicism; that is, trends or styles inspired by the revisiting of images, texts, and works of the past. In the process, the universe of modern forms was expanded and sometimes technology was affected. Such a return to "forgotten" techniques is a traditional leitmotif in the history of the *arts du feu (fire arts)* and are bound to the mythologies of alchemy. They preoccupied many 19th-century personalities far beyond the circle of industrial and decorative arts.

Before undertaking his research on glass, Henry Cros studied the finds of recent archaeological excavations and experimented with another "lost" technique: encaustic painting. In collaboration with Charles Henry (1859-1929), a librarian at the Sorbonne who was also interested in color theories, Cros published his research in 1884. He made use of his finds in two-dimensional media (encaustic painting on canvas, paper, and wood panels) as well in three-dimensional (bas-reliefs and sculptures in the round, both molded and modeled).

In the field of glassmaking, visitors to the Exposition Universelle of 1878 in Paris discovered exquisite contemporary multicolored enameled pieces derivative of Islamic art (the Mameluke tradition), as well as layered and wheel-carved glasses inspired by the *Portland Vase,* the most renowned example of Roman cameo glass. Also on view were copies of historic works sometimes called "mosaic glass" made by fusing sections of polychrome rods. It was as though the technicians of the 19th century hoped to master all of the glassmaking methods of the past—the Occident appropriates history at the same time that it colonizes the planet.

In the case of Cros, however, any desire for prowess or dominance was superseded by an aesthetic goal corresponding to contemporary artistic controversy. His objective was to rehabilitate the aesthetic status of polychrome sculpture by seeking a new and original solution that would avoid vulgar coloration and differentiate itself from the vaguely decadent preciosity of Greco-Roman and modern chryselephantine (ornate metal and ivory decoration).

The mythical and symbolic richness of historic glassmaking as outlined by Pliny and in more modern works such as Achille Deville's *Histoire de la verrerie dans l'Antiquite (History of Glassmaking in Antiquity* [1871]), fascinated Cros. His family came from Narbonne, a Gallo-Roman city in the south of France, and Cros would contribute a Mediterranean vein to the European-wide (mainly Germanic) campaign for the rehabilitation of polychrome sculpture. In 1917, the sculptor Emile Bourdelle described the Mediterranean essence of Cros's work by writing, *"L'Egypte y calcule, la Syrie y décore, la Gréce y sculpte en frémissant et toute une France y sourit. Telle fut l'oeuvre d'Henry Cros, toute l'Antiquité dans une âme nouvelle."* ("The calculation of Egypt is there, the decoration of Syria is there, Greek sculpture is there and all of France smiles on it. Such was the work of Henry Cros, all of Antiquity in a new soul.")

In 1883, Cros first associated the expression *pâte de verre* with his name in the catalogue of the annual, and at that time, unique Salon where he exhibited in the section of *gravure en médaille* (medallions). He showed a portrait of *Madame A.* that he specifically described as *pâte de verre coloré* [the word *coloré* (colored) agrees with *verre*, not with *pâte*]. Cros did not invent the term for what he regarded as a revival—he chose it from the vocabulary of antiquarians, explaining that it was an expression "used by collectors for glass objects in relief and colored in several tones." Journalists of the time quickly associated this vague and general terminology with the lineage of the *Portland Vase*, as well as with antique *diatretum* (cage cups), and most surprisingly, with mosaic glass and the antique and alchemical myth of *verre mou*, an unbreakable soft glass that could be hammered into a form while in a cold state.

The degree of confusion in Cros's mind regarding these matters is not clear, but we can be sure that he believed he had rediscovered not one technique, but a general principle from which different mysterious or misunderstood techniques originated. In one of his notebooks he even briefly referred to the secrets of Chinese glass despite the lack of information about this subject at the time. Nor do we know if Cros was aware of the small glass powder objects molded in "plaster of Paris" and made in England by James Tassie (1735-1799), and then William Tassie (1777-1860). We are also not sure if he was familiar with the term *pâte d'émeraude* (emerald paste) given in 1697 by Haudicquer de Blancourt to a formula for glass imitations of precious stones. It is probable, however, that it was through the tradition of forging gems and antiquities that certain links with practices of the past were established.

From 1883 to 1897, Cros was the only artist-glassmaker-ceramist using *pâte de verre*. At first his work was subsidized by a private patron, then after the Exposition Universelle of 1889 he received support from the State. Cros was supplied with an annual financial grant, awarded important government commissions, and given a

**Figure: 1**

Henry Cros (1840-1907)
France
*la source gelée et le soleil,* first sketch for the earliest known piece of symbolist *pâte de verre* by Henry Cros, 1884-1885 (the object was fabricated in 1885, after state acquisition it was allocated to the Musée Adrien Dubouché, Limoges, France)
Watercolor and ink on paper
H. (max.) 8"
Private collection, Paris
Photo: courtesy of the author

**Figure: 2**

Henry Cros (1840-1907)
France
*la verrerie antique,* 1888
*Pâte de verre*
10 1/4" x 8"
Collection of the Musée national
Adrien Dubouché, Limoges
Photo: courtesy of the author

**Figure: 3**

Henry Cros (1840-1907)
France
*l'Histoire du feu
(The Story-History of Fire),* 1900
Photo: installation at the Musée
des Arts Décoratifs, Paris, in 1994
*Pâte de verre*
H. (max) 71"
Collection of the Musée des Arts
Décoratifs, Paris
Photo: courtesy of the author

workspace on the grounds of the national porcelain enterprise, the Manufacture de Sèvres.

At the Salon of 1885 Cros exhibited his first *pâte de verre* object with a symbolist theme. Entitled *la source gelée et le soleil* (preserved in the museum Adrien Dubouché in Limoges), this small bas-relief associated a traditional mythological subject, the chariot of Phoebus (the sun), with a girl stretching while awakening— a living source thawing in the spring sun and returning to life, akin to the cycle of time and the transformation of matter. Like the painter Puvis de Chavannes (with whom he was often associated), Cros created new symbols which he mixed with the ancient ones. As in *les dieux antiques*, a free adaptation of the book by G. W. Cox published in French in 1880 by the poet Stephane Mallarmé, Greco-Roman mythology is interpreted by Cros as a metaphor of nature, the seasons, and the stages of life. Cros's watercolor study for the piece (Figure 1) already displays the principles and fundamental themes of his ensuing work with glass, even though the fusing and coloration methods were yet to be perfected.

In 1888 Cros named a new bas-relief *la verrerie antique* (Figure 2). Here we see, as represented by Cros, the image of rejuvenation through the fountain of youth. The famous archeological treasure, the Roman funerary vase which bears the name of the Duchess of Portland, is studied in silent meditation by a nude young woman whom one can see as a personification of Cros's *pâte de verre*: a youthful classical, but sensual, beauty. Like the mythical phoenix, ancient glassmaking is reborn from the ashes. Here again, the cycles of time, the force and the beauty of silence, and the mythologies of fire are the keys to the imaginary universe of Cros. Elsewhere, like many symbolist painters and sculptors, Cros presents the allegory of silence in the form of an enigmatic woman with her finger to her mouth, like the Greek god Harpocrate.

Two monumental masterpieces that occupied the majority of Cros's time from 1893 until 1900 are bas-reliefs on the themes of *l'Histoire de l'eau (The Story-History of Water)* [1894, H. 90", collection of the Musée d'Orsay, Paris] and the *l'Histoire du Feu (The Story-History of Fire)* [Figure 3]. The first takes as its central motif "the source" which melts in the sun and develops like a narrative musical theme leading the viewer to the ocean. It recalls the ambitious work by the artist's brother, Charles Cros (1842-1888), a poem called *le fleuve (The River)*, that was illustrated by the painter Edouard Manet.

With his *l'Histoire du feu*, Cros tackled all of Promethean mythology. The composition diffuses like heat around the central figure, again in the form of a young woman, the "flame" between Pallas Athena and Prometheus. Cros's mask exhibited in Paris in 1900 (Figures 4 and 5) is probably another allegory of fire. The only other known molding of this mask is in the collection of the Musée Boulogne sur Mer. It is sometimes called *The Gold Mine*, most probably because of the copper crystals (aventurine) in the hair that were formed by the reduction of oxygen in the kiln during the firing.

His last work, unfinished when Cros died in 1907 and allegedly completed by his son Jean (1882-1932), was a fireplace—another symbol of fire—whose central panel evokes "the hope of a beautiful season"—another of Cros's references to the cyclical nature of time. It would become a key theme in early modern art and come to fruition in Henri Matisse's 1907 painting *luxe, calme, et volupté*. Another imaginary theme that one can find consistently in Cros starting as early as 1888 is the transformation of matter. The physical fusing of glass echoes the movement between water and ice, and according to legend, the metamorphosis of blood into coral, as exemplified in Cros's *Head of Medusa* exhibited in 1907.

Cros never sought transparency or even translucency in glass and he never polished his pieces after removing them from the molds. His glass, therefore, is neither brilliant nor sparkling; surfaces are matte and the grains of glass are tightly compacted creating an extremely sensual texture. The subtle colors radiate over the surface of this substance that is opaque, but not completely impenetrable to light.

Cros's aesthetic does not display the extremes of expression or the motley assortment of colors that offended the "good taste" of contemporary detractors of polychrome sculpture. Those individuals were the followers of a lingering, but still dominant, classicism. However, a second sculptor who used *pâte de verre*, "a Parisian to the end of his fingernails" although of Alsatian origin, was a perfect representative of the style of orientalism (in the sense of rich and gilded)—the "exhibitionist" branch of polychrome sculpture. Jean Désiré Ringel D'Ilzach [hence referred to as Ringel] (1847-1916) was most widely known for the life-size busts in polychrome wax that he created from 1878. A group from 1897 symbolized the nine symphonies of Beethoven.

In 1897, in the town of Sèvres (but not at the Manufacture Nationale), Ringel and a long-time acquaintance, the famous ceramicist, Albert Dammouse (1848-1926), experimented with the molding of glass in refractory ceramic molds. It was, therefore, the joint efforts of a specialist in metallurgy (Ringel had registered patents for bronze) and a specialist in ceramics and enamels (Dammouse was the son of a decorator at the Manufacture National de Sèvres) that would eventually reveal the "secrets" of Cros's *pâte de verre*. At the Salon de la Société Nationale des Beaux-Arts (SNBA) of 1898, Ringel exhibited one of his specialties—portrait medallions such as the one depicting poet Maurice Rollinat—made in what he called *émaux agglomérés* (compressed enamels).

**Figure: 4**

Henry Cros (1840-1907)
France
Mask, *la flamme*, exhibited in the Exposition Universelle, Paris, 1900
*Pâte de verre* (powders and frit)
12 5/8" x 6 3/4" x 2";
Photo: Laurent-Sully Jaulmes
Anonymous loan

**Figure: 5**

A selection of objects exhibited by Henry Cros at the Exposition Universelle, Paris, 1900
From E. Baumgarte,
*La Manufacture Nationale de Sèvres à l'Exposition, Paris,*
Librairie Centrale des Beaux Arts, 1900

In spite of his contacts with the glass manufacturer Saint Gobain and later with the Cristallerie Saint-Louis, Ringel did not leave a legacy in glass as original and personal as that of Cros, and his polychrome work is mainly related to wax and stoneware. While this text cannot dwell on him, Ringel is an important figure in glass and his work is rare. It is thanks to him that the technical principles of *pâte de verre*, which Henry Cros taught only to his son Jean, began their dissemination.

As early as 1897 Dammouse exhibited small precious glass objects which he sometimes called *pâte d'émail* (enamel paste). In the case of both Ringel and Dammouse, the use of terms other than *pâte de verre* was more likely a way of avoiding conflict with Henry Cros than to specify a variation of the technique. None of them, however, ever revealed their variations of the glass formulas and the basic techniques.

A real and original harmony appears in Dammouse's glass by 1902 in the form of his fragile cups, no thicker than an eggshell, with elegant detailed profiles. The floral works that he exhibited from 1910 through 1912 were made by molding real petals from tulips or irises. Representative of the late Art Nouveau, they are among the most subtle masterpieces of the Parisian view of the organic ornamentation pioneered by Emile Gallé in the city of Nancy. However, one of the most important differences between these artists is that Gallé would never have made a mold from a natural object.

At the Exposition Universelle of Paris in 1900, an engineer and expert in industrial glassmaking, Georges Despret (1862-1952), first exhibited the results of his technical experiments conducted in a workshop at the factories of Boussois in northern France (near Sars-Poteries). Despret was an "editor" of modern decorative items such as his reinterpretations and modernizations of the Greek "Tanagra" figures. He also supervised the production of other decorative items such as masks of fashionable Parisian women and small "stained glass" panels for table decoration. The repertoire of Despret's workshop, which seems to have been the first to successfully produce limited editions of designs in *pâte de verre*, also included large quantities of cups and other small objects in simple shapes. The principle innovations added by Despret to the general corpus of *pâte de verre* are the translucency and vivid hues apparent in some of his pieces. Also, his collaboration with sculptors of the day, including Alexandre Charpentier, set an important precedent.

The leading figure in the world of *pâte de verre* who appeared just after 1900 was François-Émile Décorchemont (1880-1971). He was the son of a sculptor who was also interested in polychrome sculpture, and the grandfather of today's artists Antoine and Etienne Leperlier. Décorchemont graduated in 1900 from the École des Arts Décoratifs of Paris, where his father taught. He worked in ceramics before exhibiting his first *pâte de verre* in 1903 in the Salon of the newly formed Société

**Figure: 6**

Group of *pâte de verre* objects by Georges Despret (four pieces, on the left) and François-Émile Décorchemont (three pieces on the right, all "*pâtes fines*")
Art et Décoration, 1907

des Artistes Décorateurs (SAD). It is impossible in this short introduction to French *pâte de verre* from 1883 to 1930 to detail the richness and the variety of Décorchemont's contributions to the fields of *pâte de verre*, stained glass, and other types of art. Interested readers are referred to an important monograph on the subject by Veronique Ayroles to be published in 2006.

After an early collaboration with his father, Décorchemont began working with a small team of two to three technical assistants in his studio. Even when executing the huge order for the windows of the church of Sainte-Odile in Paris from 1934 to 1938, Décorchemont never employed more than ten workers. For this reason, his private workshop (unsubsidized by the government, nor any university or industry) in his native village of Conches in Normandy, and the studio of the glassblower Jean Sala (1895-1976), located in heart of Paris, are models of the Studio Glass concept which was developed, but not invented, in the United States during the 1960s. It should be noted that Jean Sala also occasionally worked in *pâte de verre*, as it is defined for this exhibition.

The position of Amalric Walter (1870-1959) is a different one. Walter was a student at the school of the Manufacture Nationale de Sèvres just before Gabriel Argy-Rousseau and Jean Cros, and as early as 1902 he exhibited several remarkable sculptures in *pâte de verre*. Only one example of his very early work is known to us and it is a superb life-size bust from a model by the sculptor Eugène Delagrange. Walter's later hyperrealist glass bestiary was influenced by the mythical model of the ceramics of Bernard Palissy (1510-1540), the protestant, humanist, scholar, and artist—a figure of monumental importance in the history of French *arts de feu*.

In later years, Walter was responsible for the creation of the first *pâte de verre* workshop integrated within a luxury glass operation, that of the Daum brothers in Nancy where Walter settled around 1904. Because his association with Daum (1904 to 1914) was not very profitable, the partners separated amicably and Walter set up a new workshop in the same city in 1918. Daum was the only decorative glass company to manufacture *pâte de verre* from 1904 to 1914; it restarted its *pâte de verre* production in 1968 and brought the technique to international attention.

The last to arrive in this marathon of *pâte de verre* from symbolism to Art Deco was Gabriel Argy-Rousseau (1885-1953). Also trained in Sèvres, his experiments and first pieces of *pâte de verre* in 1914 were influenced by the technical achievements of Henry Cros. Argy-Rousseau's mature work developed after World War I, mainly between 1921 and 1931, thanks to the production and marketing of his designs by the Moser brothers, famous glassmakers in Karlový Vary (Karlsbad), Czechoslovakia. Part of the Moser family was based in Paris and operated the successful Moser-Millot gallery there.

Argy-Rousseau's work was typical of the new taste for the antique as envisioned and modified by Parisian theatrical and cabaret productions. His most important contributions to the field of *pâte de verre* are in jewelry (pendants mounted with cords of colored silk thread) and decorative lighting—particularly his famous night lights which created a warm and intimate effect. Argy-Rousseau's *pâte de verre* is translucent and semi-polished; neither looking as fragile as Dammouse's, nor as massive as Décorchemont's later work. In short, he brought *pâte de verre* back to the more traditional repertory of the glassmaker.

Argy-Rousseau was also a brilliant technician and we know more about his working methods than the other early practitioners. Some of his papers were sold by the Mosers to the library of The Corning Museum of Glass and, as Susanne Frantz reminds us in her essay, they influenced a later generation of British artists. Included among that group is Diana Hobson who, early in her glassmaking career, spent an afternoon in the Musée des Arts Décoratifs in Paris where she was fascinated by the very rich Dammouse collection. Hobson then paid a visit to the Leperlier brothers who had exhibited their work at the museum for the first time in 1982 as part of the *Verriers Français Art et Industrie* exhibition (organized to coincide with the French venue of Corning's *New Glass*). In such ways, "the secrets of *pâte de verre*"—which were, in truth, no longer secrets—were propagated more easily and in a different way after 1930.

During its first fifty years, *pâte de verre* remained a very delicate and difficult technique developed through individual experimentation. It favored forms and colors that were much more subtle and varied than those of today. In this era of globalization in which catalogs of industrial refractories, raw materials, and colors are available by e-mail, glass has a certain similarity. This exhibition, in the hands of a demanding and competent guest curator, Susanne Frantz, shows us that if glass can be molded today almost like "ordinary" bronze, plaster, or plastic, *pâte de verre* (or one should say *pâtes de verre*) can once again be a field of intellectual and artistic research, full of surprises, and offering a remarkable wellspring of adventure for some *artistes verriers*.

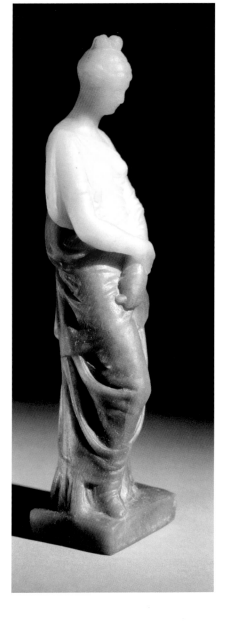

FROM ABOVE CLOCKWISE

**Figure: 7**

Georges Despret (1862–1952)
France
Bust of a Woman, about 1905
*Pâte de verre* (powder and frit)
4 3/4" x 2 1/4" x 2 1/2"
Gift of Lillian Nassau Ltd.
Collection of
The Corning Museum of Glass

**Figure: 8**

Georges Despret (1862–1952)
France
*Seahorse Vase,* about 1906
*Pâte de verre* (powder and frit)
8 1/4" x Diam. (rim) 3 1/2"
Gift of Walter P. Chrysler, Jr.
Collection of the Chrysler Museum of Art,
Norfolk, VA

**Figure: 9**

Georges Despret (1862–1952)
France
*Tanagra Figure* (after ancient Hellenistic
molded ceramics), about 1906
*Pâte de verre* (powder and frit;
lost wax mold)
11" x 2 1/4" x 2 3/4"
Gift of Walter P. Chrysler, Jr.
Collection of the Chrysler Museum of Art,
Norfolk, VA

**Figure: 10**

Georges Despret (1862–1952)
France
*Fish,* about 1906, after a design by
Yvonne Serruys (1873-1953)
*Pâte de verre* (powder and frit)
H. 10"
Gift of Walter P. Chrysler, Jr.
Collection of the Chrysler Museum of Art,
Norfolk, VA

**Figure: 11**

François-Émile Décorchemont
(1880–1971)
France
Vase with beetles, 1905-1912
*Pâte de verre* (powder and fine frit;
lost wax mold)
5 1/4" x Diam. 4 1/4"
Courtesy of Barry Friedman, Ltd.

**Figure: 13**

François-Émile Décorchemont
(1880–1971)
France
Vase with masks, 1913-1918
*Pâte de verre* (powder and fine frit;
lost wax mold)
9 1/4" x Diam. (rim) 2"
Gift of Walter P. Chrysler, Jr.
In honor of Reneé Diamonstein
Collection of the Chrysler Museum of Art,
Norfolk, VA

**Figure: 12**

François-Émile Décorchemont
(1880–1971)
France
Vase with shells, aquatic plants, and
seahorse, about 1912
*Pâte de verre* (powder and fine frit;
lost wax mold)
7 1/4" x Diam. 4 1/2"
Courtesy of Barry Friedman, Ltd.

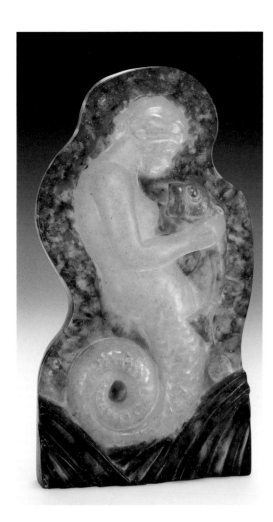

**Figure: 14**

François-Émile Décorchemont (1880–1971)
France
*Sirène au Poisson*, made for a fountain
on the Champs Elysées, Paris, about 1936
*Pâte de verre* (powder and frit;
lost wax mold)
13" x 7 1/4" x 2"
Collection of
The Corning Museum of Glass

**Figure: 15**

René Lalique (1860–1945)
France
Pendant with two birds, about 1905
*Pâte de verre*; enamel, copper backing, baroque pearl
W. 4 7/16"
Gift by exchange with
Mr. and Mrs. Glenn S. Utt, Jr.
Collection of
The Corning Museum of Glass

**Figure: 16**

René Lalique (1860–1945)
France
Design for pendant with two birds,
about 1905
Pencil, ink, watercolor on paper
Original: 10 7/16" x 8 1/2"
Collection of the Rakow Research Library,
The Corning Museum of Glass

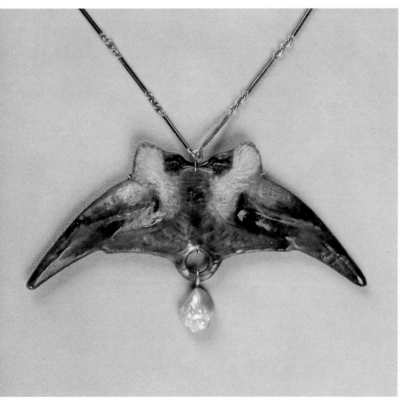

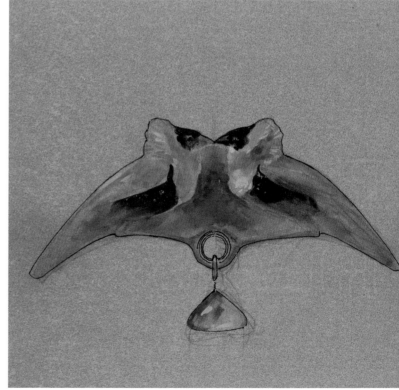

**Figure: 17**

Jules-Paul Brateau (1844-1923)
France
Floral-Design Cup, 1910-1912
*Pâte de verre* (pastes of powder
and fine frit)
2 1/2" x Diam. (rim) 3 1/4"
Gift of Walter P. Chrysler, Jr.
Collection of the Chrysler Museum of Art,
Norfolk, VA

**Figure: 18**

Jules-Paul Brateau (1844-1923)
France
Box, about 1910
*Pâte de verre* (pastes of powder
and fine frit)
L. 3 3/4"
Collection of the Chrysler Museum of Art,
Norfolk, VA

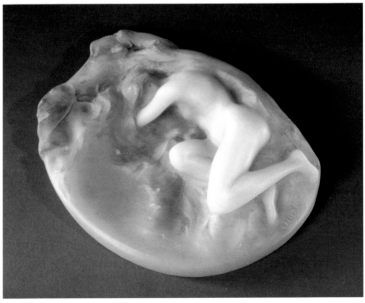

**Figure: 19**

Albert Louis Dammouse (1848–1926)
France
Vase with seaweed, about 1910
*Pâte de verre* (pastes of powder and frit)
4 3/4" x Diam. 4 1/8"
Gift of The Hon. and Mrs. Amory Houghton
Collection of The Corning Museum of Glass

**Figure: 20**

Victor Amalric Walter (1870-1959)
France
*Reclining Nude* paperweight, about 1920
*Pâte de verre* (pastes of powder and frit)
2 1/8" x 6 1/4" x 9"
Gift of Walter P. Chrysler, Jr.
Collection of the Chrysler Museum of Art,
Norfolk, VA

FROM ABOVE CLOCKWISE

## Figure: 21

Victor Amalric Walter (1870-1959)
France
*Dragonfly vide poche*, about 1920,
designed by Henri Bergé (1870-1930)
*Pâte de verre* (powders and frit)
1 5/8" x Diam. 7 7/8"
Gift of Walter P. Chrysler, Jr.
Collection of the Chrysler Museum of Art,
Norfolk, VA

## Figure: 22

Victor Amalric Walter (1870-1959)
France
*Chameleon vide poche*, about 1920,
designed by Henri Bergé (1870-1930)
*Pâte de verre* (powders and frit)
3 1/16" x 3"
Gift of Walter P. Chrysler, Jr.
Collection of the Chrysler Museum of Art,
Norfolk, VA

## Figure: 23

Joseph-Gabriel Argy-Rousseau
(1885–1953)
France
*Danseuse* (dancer Loïe Fuller),
about 1925-1930, designed by
Marcel Bouraine (1886-1948)
*Pâte de verre* (powder and lead frit,
called "*pâte de cristal*" by Argy-Rousseau;
lost wax mold)
9 3/4" x 3 3/4" x 5 1/2" (wings)
Collection of
The Corning Museum of Glass

## Figure: 24

Joseph-Gabriel Argy-Rousseau
(1885–1953)
France
*Farniente Vase,* about 1927
*Pâte de verre* (pastes of powder and frit;
lost wax mold)
6" x 4" x 5"
Gift of Walter P. Chrysler, Jr
Collection of the Chrysler Museum of Art,
Norfolk, VA

## Figure: 25

Joseph-Gabriel Argy-Rousseau
(1885–1953)
France
*Wolves in the Snow Vase,* about 1925
*Pâte de verre* (powders and frit;
lost wax mold)
9 5/16" x Diam. (rim) 4 3/4"
Gift of Walter P. Chrysler, Jr.
Collection of the Chrysler Museum of Art,
Norfolk, VA

# *Pâte de Verre*: The Beautiful Conundrum

By Susanne K. Frantz

P*âte de verre* is a technique for shaping glass by fusing granulated glass (frit) in molds. Visually, it stands in stark contrast to all other forms of the medium and is the antithesis of the blown bubble of brilliantly hued or absolutely colorless material so associated with modern glass. It can imitate carved semi-precious stones such as lapis lazuli, jade, and turquoise; mimicry is a tradition steeped in glass history from its beginnings centuries before the appearance of perfectly transparent and colorless blown glass. Because the technique has several variations and ways of being finished, *pâte de verre* may be as light and thin as eggshell or as massive and dense as rock; it may appear pliable and waxy, or crystalline, like hoarfrost; textures may be porous and gritty, or smooth and shining; color detail is placed with precision or allowed to freely striate the inside and outside of the form.

As glass, *pâte de verre* always has a degree of internal illumination that may be perceived in even those works of maximum density. Its glow can replicate the sensation of living flora and fauna, skin and flesh, and embodies a multitude of metaphors for the body and spirit. Turn-of-the-century artists influenced by the luminescence of symbolist and late Impressionist painting turned to *pâte de verre* as a means of creating three-dimensional, colored interpretations of the styles. Sculptor Auguste Rodin was a long-time admirer of Henry Cros (credited with the late 19th-century revival of what was probably an ancient technique) and was tempted by the idea of casting objects in a permanent medium with varying degrees of translucency and porousness suggesting marble. Around 1911-1912, some of Rodin's sculptures (most notably, a portrait of Camille Claudel) were executed in *pâte de verre* by Cros's son, Jean, who also cast some objects for the sculptor Antoine Bourdelle in 1922.[1]

Just what is *pâte de verre*? The seemingly small question of definition has confounded everyone who has ever attempted to explain one of the most intriguing ways to sculpt with glass. Every aspect of the technique—from terminology, to particle sizes and shapes, to mold types and how they are filled and fired—is subject to different, strongly held points of view. While *pâte de verre* is a type of cast glass, the term "cast" enfolds molded glass in any state, including glass "slumped" over or into a form and molten glass ladled into a mold. The situation boils down to something like the old saying about the difference between Scotch and whiskey—that is, all Scotch is whiskey, but not all whiskey is Scotch. Likewise, it is true that all *pâte de verre* is cast glass, but not all cast glass is *pâte de verre*—and somewhere, someone is already disputing that simple statement.

For the past one hundred years, artists, craftspersons, curators, dealers, and collectors have debated the correct use of the term and applied it rather indiscriminately. The truth is that there has never been a single, absolute definition of *pâte de verre*. Research by the technique's leading expert, Jean-Luc Olivié, has shown that in the 1880s even Henry Cros applied the pre-existing term to a range of polychrome sculptural glass objects made by a variety of techniques. We know that for much of his work Cros fused fine glass powders in molds, however, no documentation exists as to his exact methods. Near the end of his life, the first modern artist in glass, Emile Gallé (1846-1904), used the term once or twice to refer to what are believed to have been nearly opaque colored glasses worked at the furnace. The name translated as "glass paste" may be interpreted as a poetic, rather than technical, descriptive. Olivié points out that it has connotations of an imaginary and mythological substance—the dream of soft glass.

The pioneering artist/craftspersons used a variety of working methods and kept their hard won information to themselves. The core argument centers on two basic ways of molding and firing granulated glass. The first method, as the name implies, employs finely ground glass powders and frits mixed with a binder to form a liquid slip or a paste (with a consistency ranging from thick cream to toothpaste), which is used to build up a thin lining in a mold. The glass is heated until it fuses, but not until it flows [see pieces by Diana Hobson and Alicia Lomné]. The second approach uses wet or dry powders and frits packed in a mold and fired and/or filled by melting the frit in an upper reservoir until it flows down and fills the cavity [the sculptures of Anja Isphording and Heinrich Wang, for example]. Coloring agents such as powdered metallic oxides and ceramic and metal enamels are positioned on the mold surface or blended in the frit. These methods are traditionally sheltered under the umbrella term of *pâte de verre*, and although it may not make sense—historically, it has not been necessary for glass particles to be made into a paste to create *pâte de verre*.

**For the purposes of this project, basic *pâte de verre* is broadly defined as: pre-melted glass reduced to a granular consistency, placed in a refractory mold, fired in a kiln until fused or melted, cooled and annealed, and then freed from the mold.**

The subtitle of this exhibition includes the words "other cast glass granulations" for good reason, and not (only) to weasel out of delivering an indisputable definition. The phrase acknowledges the ever-expanding field of artistic objects incorporating glass particles fused in different ways, combined with other glassmaking techniques and materials.

# The Process and the Debates

This text will not end the search for a pat definition, nor is it meant to serve as a do-it-yourself guide to making *pâte de verre*. Although it was not always so, such information is readily available today in classes, books, and other resources such as those found in the Rakow Research Library of The Corning Museum of Glass. However, to summarize the process: *pâte de verre* is formed in a hollow mold that is fired in a kiln. The mold making process is as critical, and equally or more complicated than the subsequent formation of the glass. There are many ways to make a mold and they are affected by any number of factors, including the complexity of the shape and the number of duplicates to be made from the original model. In general, a model positive is encased (invested) in a refractory material that can withstand relatively high temperatures. The model may be made of almost any substance, but is often a flexible material such as clay, wax, rubber, Styrofoam, or a combination thereof. Once the refractory has solidified around the model, the model is removed, leaving its negative impression. Although only one piece of *pâte de verre* may be made from a single mold, multiple duplicate molds may be made from an original model.

To reduce stress on the mold, the glasses used for *pâte de verre* must melt at relatively low temperatures and sometimes contain lead. The raw ingredients in a glass recipe require too high of a temperature to melt in the mold, therefore, the glass for *pâte de verre* is always pre-made. By pre-melting, the glass is "fluxed down" to soften at a lower temperature.[2] Once cooled, the solidified glass is broken down (by heat-fracturing, machine milling, or with hand tools including mortar and pestle) to create granules and powders. The frit is cleansed of impurities and separated according to size by sifting through graduated screens. In the not too distant past, artists who did not melt their own glass from raw ingredients had to search for suitable materials from industrial sources. For example, Diana Hobson made her frits from tubing used in the light bulb industry. Today, many makers avoid part of the tedious process by purchasing ready-made powders and frits or glass beads (such as those used for highway marking). It should be noted that the eventual availability of frits with compatible coefficients of expansion developed by the Bullseye Glass Company in Portland, Oregon, and Gaffer Glass in New Zealand, have been an important factor in increasing the popularity of *pâte de verre* making.

Depending on the particle sizes and shapes, the way the glass is placed in the mold, and the extent to which it is melted, the look of the finished object may range from translucent to milky, to almost opaque—even in a single piece. The smaller the glass grain and the more spherical its shape, the more opaque the finished glass. That is because each grain is surrounded by air; smaller, more rounded particles trap more minute air bubbles in between them, even when they melt, than do larger or more irregular pieces. Cast glass that is the most pellucid (i.e. with the fewest bubbles) is obtained by melting one or more blocks (billets) of high quality glass into the mold and also by firing to a high temperature.[3]

Today, almost all *pâte de verre* is made in electric kilns, however, those of the early pioneers were fueled by gas or oil (Figure 26). Décorchemont's primitive furnace burned a petroleum that was refined for lighting.[4] It is not easy to successfully fuse or melt glass in a mold; glass has narrow fusion thresholds and the degree and duration of firing schedules must be carefully controlled. Too much heat can cause the glass to bubble and "boil over," forcing the colors to run together and the shape to distort. With too little heat, the glass particles do not vitrify and will fall apart. The mold must also withstand the stresses inflicted on it by both the heat and the glass; cracking is a common problem. To make matters worse, a malfunctioning kiln or an unexpected loss of electricity can spoil a piece that has taken weeks to make.

**Figure: 26**
Gabriel Argy-Rousseau placing a mold in his kiln around 1928.

Once the fired mold and glass have survived the firing and slowly cooled to room temperature, the now solidified glass is carefully coaxed from the mold, and in the process, the "waste mold" is destroyed. The freed glass can be left with a chalky or matte surface caused from contact with the mold and its residue. The parts of the glass that did not touch the mold are smooth and "fire polished." The glass is cleaned and finished by using a variety of coldworking techniques such as grinding, sandblasting, acid etching, cutting, engraving, and polishing. Re-firings further manipulate the form, coloration, and surface texture, and can join separately molded components and correct any flaws.

## Two Methods - Both *Pâte de Verre*

Much of the debate around *pâte de verre* is rooted in the two quite different approaches to the molding and firing processes. The differences between them, as well as the numerous finishing techniques, explain why *pâte de verre* has such a wide range of appearances. The first method usually employs an "open" mold—that is, a mold in a shape that is fully accessible to the hand of the artist, like a shell or a bowl. While the mold may be highly detailed, there is enough of an opening so that the artist may reach inside with a tool to place the glass with precision.

An open mold may be lined or filled with dry powders and frits (see Aufiero, Figures 47, 48), but it is also used with glass slips and pastes applied layer-by-layer

*On opposite page:*

**Figure: 27**
Large bowl of glass frit with a smaller bowl of glass powder on top.

**Figure: 28**
Applying the glass paste to the open mold.

**Figure: 29**
Compacting the final layer of glass.

**Figure: 30**
The covered mold in the kiln.

**Figure: 31**
Cleaning the glass after firing and removal from the mold.

to build up a mold lining. While applying the layers, the artist is working from the outside to the inside of the form; typically, color is placed first in the mold details, then backed up with larger particles. The damp or wet mixtures result from mixing the particles with a binder that may be almost anything including water, gum arabic, oil of lavender, or organic glue. Some artists use such humble substances as honey, hand lotion, mashed quince pips, and cough syrup. Wallpaper paste is one of the best binders due to its ready availability, low cost, and the fact that when it burns out during the firing it does not leave a residue. The mold material is kept damp and its moisture helps the glass to stay in place and keeps the colors delineated from one another. As the glass mixture is brushed, tamped, pushed, or packed in the mold, it is frequently compressed to force out as much air as possible and to reduce shrinkage and movement. This branch of *pâte de verre* has much in common with Egyptian paste, faience, and porcelain making, and in the past the misleading term *pâte d'émail* (Fr., enamel paste), was sometimes applied to it. This series of photos taken of Diana Hobson working in 1985 and 1986 shows several steps in the process (Figures 27-31).

Much of the European work from the first half of the 20th century was also made by a second method using a "closed" mold—one with areas that may not be accessible by the hand or tools. This method is particularly appropriate for thicker objects and those made in complex shapes and with many undercuts. The mold is packed solid with particles and placed in the kiln. The larger the particles of glass, the more the glass will settle and compact as it melts, causing it to lose up to one-half of its volume. To make sure that the mold remains adequately filled, supplemental frit is either mounded at the mold opening or added a little at a time during the firing. It may also be held in an upper reservoir (constructed as part of the mold, or a simple terracotta flowerpot sitting on top) and melted into the mold. As trapped air is displaced and escapes through straw-like sprues, it is replaced by glass flowing into the nooks and crannies of the mold and filling any air pockets. It is also possible to fill the mold solely with glass flowing down from the reservoir rather than using it only to "top off" the pre-packed frit. The second variation of *pâte de verre* is sometimes christened with yet another misleading name—*cire perdue* or lost wax.

Lost wax is a moldmaking technique, not a glassmaking technique, and was developed for the casting of metals. To make a lost wax mold, a wax model is invested and then removed by heating until the wax melts, burns, or steams out, leaving a mold cavity that is an exact negative of the original model. The wax that is "lost" during the process gives the technique its name. François-Émile Décorchemont, one of the greatest practitioners, called all of his work *pâte de verre*, whether it was made with pastes lining an open mold or by melting frit in a lost wax mold. Muddying the waters further, both René Lalique in France, and Frederick Carder, co-founder of Steuben Glass in Corning, New York, began calling the entire technique (not just the mold) "cire perdue" during the 1920s. In all fairness, they were probably attempting to differentiate between the various methods, but the result was the mistaken use of a moldmaking term for a glassmaking technique. The fact is that it is possible to fill a lost wax mold in any number of ways, including blowing glass into it.

The matter of appropriate particle size is another part of the *pâte de verre* controversy and raises the question: At what diameter does a glass particle turn from powder into frit? And because there is a relatively wide range of frit diameters, when does a coarse frit become a small piece of cullet? The sales catalogue of the Bullseye Glass Company offers the following grades of particles: **powder** (at times called "powdered frit," 0.2 mm or less in diameter); **fine** (0.2-1.2 mm, the approximate consistency of coarsely granulated sugar); **medium** (1.2-2.7 mm, the approximate size of a sesame seed); and **coarse** (2.7-5.2 mm, slightly smaller than a lentil). Gaffer Glass has comparable groups called talc and grain powders, plus three sizes of "chips." The term "cullet" is a broad term for almost any size of fragmented glass; Bullseye categorizes theirs as measuring from 1.5 x 1.5 cm to 1.5 x 15.2 cm.

# The Terms

The search for appropriate terminology has been a mission since Henry Cros adopted the name of *pâte de verre* at the end of the 19th century. His contemporaries and those immediately following tried out other descriptives such as *grès verre* and *émaux agglomérés* (used by Jean-Désiré Ringel d'Ilzach), *pâte d'émail* (for the small and delicate glass paste vessels by Albert-Louis Dammouse and François-Émile Décorchemont), and *pâte de cristal* (used by Gabriel Argy-Rousseau for more translucent *pâte de verre* made with lead glass).

At the height of the international *pâte de verre* revival in the 1980s, it was not uncommon for almost any type of molded glass to be called *pâte de verre*. After much outcry and soul searching, today's artists are not so quick to use the label and have coined new and more specific terms. For example, Toots Zynsky called her pulled and fused strands of glass *filet de verre*. The past ten years have seen the proliferation of *frit-cast, fuse-cast, kiln-cast, lost-wax cast, kiln-fused, kiln-formed, mold-melted,* and even *drip-cast* and *glass slip-cast*. While most of the terms stem from a sincere desire to descramble the dialogue, their inconsistent application and redundancy have added a new chapter of confusion. One can ask at what point does *pâte de verre* change to frit-cast or kiln-cast, and then to mold-melted (the term used by many of the Czech artists who melt finger- or fist-size pieces of glass in molds)? While no one would refer to the Czech technique as *pâte de verre*, it is only a matter of particle size that distinguishes one subgroup from the other. What is next, *frit de verre* and *pâte de cullet*? In the words of Antoine Leperlier,

"We move from *pâte de verre* to kiln-casting—from Diana Hobson to Stanislav Libenský—just by changing the size of the frit."

As the final nail in the coffin, what if a mold is not used at all? Some of the early French *pâte de verre* was described in contemporary literature as being fired without a mold. Artist Charissa Brock in Portland, Oregon calls her process *patisserie de verre* and explains it as follows: "Dry frit is sifted over a petal-shaped stencil directly onto the kiln shelf. The stencil is removed and the frit petals are fired. After cooling, the wafers are slumped by refiring over a mold." Catharine Newell, also in Portland, and Lada Semecka in the Czech Republic are fusing glass particles and raw silica sand, respectively, onto sheet glass. It can be argued that, in theory, their work also represents variations on *pâte de verre*.

Does anyone really care? Well, yes, if only within the small glass community. And those who do care, care a lot. The meaning of *pâte de verre* is unceasingly contested in the interest of accuracy and when the term is appropriated for seemingly less challenging ways of sculpting glass. The 1989 German exhibition, *Verschmelzungen Glas* (Fused Glass) made a noble effort to distinguish between *pâte de verre* and other kilnforming techniques, as well as closely related techniques for ceramic and enamel making.[5] The issue, however, remains unsettled.

Although the inconsistent usage of the term *pâte de verre* has historical precedent and it is probably impossible to invent a glossary that covers all of the variances and is also universally accepted, it is always useful to strive for greater clarification. The following suggestions are offered in an attempt to winnow the terms in use:

**Pâte de verre**—granulized glass in the form of powder and/or fine frit mixed with water or a binder to form a slip or a paste, placed in a mold (either lining it or filling it), and heated until fused.

**Frit-cast glass**—granular glass up to the approximate size of 5 mm (approx. ¼") in diameter, used wet or dry, packed in a mold and/or melted and flowing from a reservoir.

**Kiln-cast glass**—pieces of glass larger than 5 mm in diameter melted in the mold or flowing from a reservoir.

**Cire perdue**—used only to describe a mold made by the lost wax process.

Sensible allowances must be made for the fact that combinations of mold types, frit sizes, and methods of filling and firing the mold, are often used by an artist for a single object.

## Modern *Pâte de Verre*

All of the above represents only a cursory summary of a painstaking, labor-intensive process and provokes the next question: For all of its beauty and special attributes, why on earth would anyone today use such an archaic, demanding, and unreliable technique?

It turns out that just as at the end of the 19th century, there remain many artists drawn not only to the aesthetic qualities of *pâte de verre*, but also to its control, methodical and slow pace, subtle detailing, and the ability to make changes along the way. It is also attractive because it does not require the space, zoning, equipment, and expense of a hot glass studio. *Pâte de verre* can be made in a kitchen using a small electric test kiln running on household current. These practical considerations made it especially attractive to artists working in Japan. While the technique lends itself especially well to the making of small works, Henry Cros proved that it is possible to use *pâte de verre* for composite fountains and architectural reliefs over six feet tall. In the late 1930s, Décorchemont created church windows that had all of the advantages and size of stained glass, but were not restricted by the need for leading.

The first flowering of French *pâte de verre* lasted from Art Nouveau at the end of the 19th century through 1930s Art Moderne. The technique was taken up outside of the borders of France and Belgium and used in Sweden during the 1920s by Agnes de Frumerie. It also appeared in Japan thanks to artist Sotoichi Koshiba (1901-1973) at the Iwaki Glassworks. After studying a broken piece by Argy-Rousseau, Koshiba and chemist Yuzo Shimizu began experimentation with *pâte de verre* in 1932. Two years later, the ceramist Yāhei Ogawa joined in the collaboration and the three exhibited their work for the first time in 1936. Koshiba retired from the Iwaki Glassworks in 1956 and in 1958 he established the Koshiba Glass Craft Institute for the continued production of *pâte de verre* items such as incense burners and jewelry, as well as stained glass and mosaics.[6]

Frederick Carder saw and wrote about the work of Henry Cros in 1897 and was also greatly impressed by the *pâte de verre* display he saw at the Paris Exposition Universelle of 1900 and the 1925 Exposition International des Arts Décoratifs et Industriels Modernes.[7] Carder was also profoundly influenced by the work of French artist René Lalique. Carder began his experiments with *pâte de verre* during the late 1920s using a small electric kiln in his office/studio at the Corning Glass Works. There is no evidence that Carder ever used a binder with his glass, and works such as his *Standing Glassblower* and *Dolphins* were made by packing lost wax molds with frit and/or feeding them from a reservoir (Figures 32, 33). Carder's spectacular *diatretum*, made between 1945 and 1959, were inspired by ancient Roman carved vessels encircled by freestanding "cages" (Figure 34). Carder's late efforts occurred around the same time that several other independent artists were

**Figure: 32**
Frederick Carder (1863–1963)
United States
*Glassblower*, 1938
*Pâte de verre*, (frit; lost wax mold);
metal detail
H. 12 1/2"
Gift of Frederick Carder
Collection of
The Corning Museum of Glass

**Figure: 33**
Frederick Carder (1863–1963)
*United States*
*Dolphins*, about 1946
*Pâte de verre*, (frit; lost wax mold)
6 3/8" x 7 1/2"
Gift of Corning Glass Works
Collection of
The Corning Museum of Glass

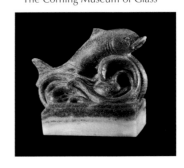

**Figure: 34**

Frederick Carder (1863–1963)
United States
*Diatreta* vessel with cover, 1953
*Pâte de verre,* (powder and frit;
lost wax mold)
10 1/8" x Diam. 8 1/2"
Gift of Frederick Carder
Collection of
The Corning Museum of Glass

**Figure: 35**

Edris Eckhardt (1910-1998)
United States
*Vernal Equinox,* 1976
*Pâte de verre* (powder and frit,
lost wax mold), originally cast
in bronze
16 1/2" x 3 1/2" x 3 1/2"
Gift of Harriet Smith
Collection of the
Museum of American Glass,
Wheaton Village

practicing variations of *pâte de verre* without knowledge of each other. During the mid-1940s and early 1950s in Czechoslovakia, artist Jaroslava Brychtová and her father, Jaroslav Brychta, were making small plaques, then vessels and sculptures from molded powders and frits. Although she spurned the term *pâte de verre,* Edris Eckhardt was working along a similar path in her basement studio in Toledo, Ohio (Figure 35); Elsa Freud in Arkansas and Frances Higgins in Illinois were also fusing crushed glass.

The early days of American Studio Glass, the 1960s and 1970s, were narrow ones in terms of definition. For the most part, Studio Glass was blown—stained glass, flameworking, kilnforming were not part of the game. A telling example in the documentation of American Studio Glass history is the dismissal of the fact that in 1962 Edris Eckhardt offered the first glassmaking class at the University of California, Berkeley. The event is seldom cited because she was teaching kilnforming rather than glassblowing. The first *Toledo Glass National* exhibition, held in 1966, was limited to work made from blown and hotworked molten glass. Occasional exceptions were made—especially for some European work and, most specifically, the cast and cut sculpture from Czechoslovakia. Even this work, which was technically and aesthetically far more sophisticated than contemporary American efforts, was saddled with the caveat "but it is made in a factory," and thus, not *really* Studio Glass. Most Czechoslovak works were indeed made using factory facilities because private studios for blowing and casting were nonexistent.

Other than the handful of artists who used variations of *pâte de verre* during the 1940s and 1950s, the technique was abandoned until the second half of the 1970s when interest was rekindled. Where could one go to learn to make *pâte de verre* from start to finish? The answer to that question is "nowhere." The words heard from the individuals who were independently researching the technique including Antoine Leperlier in France, Diana Hobson in England, and Marianne Maderna in Austria, are "trial and error."

The landmark international survey, *New Glass,* presented by The Corning Museum of Glass in 1979, attempted to reflect the cumulative state of international Studio Glass. Even with its rubbery definition of the genre (mass-produced tableware was included in the show), the exhibition represented a wide variety of techniques. Among

the smorgasbord of offerings united only by their common material, one of the most unusual was the only piece of *pâte de verre* in the show, the sculpture *Ektoplasma,* by Marianne Maderna of Vienna (Figure 36). The mysterious, life-sized representation of a female face was massive and solid—like a cross between stone and patinated bronze; instead of radiating transparent candy colors, it was a matte, mossy gold. *Ektoplasma* seemed like something from the distant past and it was plainly out of sync with the blowpipe-twirling, floppy-bubble producing, rock-and-roll disciples of American Studio Glass. Like Henry Cros, Maderna was searching for a sculptural medium that had the qualities of stone, but could be colored and modeled by hand. Maderna's account of her struggle to fuse powdered glass packed in a lost wax mold and finished with hydrofluoric acid brings to mind some epic battle. In the process, her studio was destroyed by a fire started from a pot of boiling wax and Maderna abandoned the technique thereafter.[8]

Unknown to Maderna, British artists were also experimenting with *pâte de verre*. In 1976, a *Working With Hot Glass* symposium was held at the Royal College of Art, London, and it included a presentation on mold making for kiln-fired glass by the school's Head of Glass, Martin Hunt. The technical information provided by Hunt (including the refractory mold recipe used by Frederick Carder) proved to be an important moment in the history of modern *pâte de verre* and a summary of his talk was published in the 1976 American-based Glass Art Society Journal. In 1978, a seminar focused on *pâte de verre* organized by Stuart Garfoot and Keith Cummings took place at the Royal College of Art. At that time, a copy of one of Argy-Rousseau's handwritten technical notebooks owned by the library of The Corning Museum of Glass was on loan to Martin Hunt.[9] The manuscript provided valuable data to both teachers and students and Cummings credits access to the notes as a significant contribution to the "growing sophistication of [glass] casting generally, and *pâte de verre* specifically." [10] In 1980, Hunt spoke about the

Argy-Rousseau treasure in a lecture entitled "Casting and *Pâte de Verre*" at the 1980 Glass Art Society meeting in Huntington, West Virginia. That same year there was another symposium at the Royal College of Art with the specific theme of kilnforming prompted by the publication of Cummings's landmark book, *The Technique of Glass Forming* [London: B.T. Batsford, 1980]. Cummings, a Senior Lecturer in Glass at the Stourbridge College of Art, had been researching kilnforming techniques since the late 1960s.

Beginning in 1973, Diana Hobson studied jewelry and silversmithing at the Royal College of Art and was looking for ways to incorporate glass into her metalwork. More precisely, Hobson wanted to fuse very finely crushed glass into a thin transparent sheet, like a large panel of *plique-a-jour* (enamel without the metal backing). She saw her first images of *pâte de verre* at the 1978 seminar and in 1981 she received grants from the British Crafts Council and the Camberwell College of Art to do technical research. As part of her studies, she traveled to Paris in 1982 to meet with Jean-Luc Olivié at the Musée des Arts Décoratifs, Paris. Accompanying Olivié in the museum storage rooms, Hobson was able to study the early and rare glass paste vessels by Albert Dammouse. At Olivié's suggestion, Hobson contacted Nöel Daum and also journeyed to the town of Conches to meet the brothers Antoine and Etienne Leperlier. Antoine was already working with *pâte de verre* in what had been the studio of his grandfather, François-Émile Décorchemont. From 1968 until his grandfather's death in 1971, the teenaged Antoine assisted and learned directly from Décorchemont. Etienne Leperlier later grew interested in the technique and the brothers shared the workshop from 1981 until 1996 when Antoine built his own studio. Décorchemont had used more than one branch of the *pâte de verre* process: his early cups were formed by applying glass pastes to open molds, his later, more monumental works came from lost wax molds filled with powders and frits.[11] Both brothers incorporate variations of their grandfather's techniques and sometimes melt billets into the mold from a reservoir. The rich symbolism of Antoine Leperlier's sculptures takes shape from multiple cast sections with manipulated external and internal shapes (Figure 104).

By 1983, Hobson had refined her technique of crushing tubes of lead glass to the consistency of powders and sugar granules, mixing them into pastes, and using them to line an open mold made from her clay original. Working inward from what would become the outside of the vessel, she took up to 17 hours to place the glass.

**From left to right:**

**Figure: 41**

Diana Hobson (b. 1943)
England
*Original Large Form 1.1, 1985*
*Pâte de verre* (pastes of powder and frit, ceramic glaze stains)
4 1/2" x 6" x 5 1/4"

**Figure: 42**

Diana Hobson (b. 1943)
England
*Original Large Form 2.1 (yellow), 1985*
*Pâte de verre* (pastes of powder and frit, ceramic glaze stains)
4 3/4" x 6" x 5 1/2"

**Figure: 43**

Diana Hobson (b. 1943)
England
*Progressive Series No. 5, 1986*
*Pâte de verre* (pastes of powder and frit, ceramic glaze stains); beach sand
6 1/4" x 8" x 4"
Collection of The Corning Museum of Glass

**Figure: 44**

Diana Hobson (b. 1943)
England
*Progressive Series 2.1, 1986*
*Pâte de verre* (pastes of powder and frit, ceramic glaze stains)
6" x 7 3/4" x 4"

The resulting diminutive, asymmetrical vessels appeared similar to textured porcelain and were very much in the spirit of Dammouse's floral cups made from around 1898 to 1905 (Figures 37-44.)

As was true in the past, other artists unknown to one another were working along similar lines. While a painting student at the Tyler School of Art in Philadelphia, Karla Trinkley also studied with the porcelain artist, Rudy Staffel. Trinkley was investigating the chemistry of glazes and experimenting with the links between glass and porcelain. During her first glassmaking class and as part of a history lesson, Professor Jon Clark read aloud to the class from an article about *pâte de verre*. The existence of the process was a revelation to Trinkley and around 1976 Trinkley began her own efforts at making frit using an antique, hand-powered jaw crusher and a sifting machine that she found later in a thrift store. In 1979, during her first year as a graduate student at the Rhode Island School of Design, Trinkley produced her first successful piece of *pâte de verre*, *Saturn Ring*, which was selected for *Corning's New Glass Review I*. While her ensuing series of ancient-looking vessels appear inspired by ancient Roman diatretum, Trinkley had unintentionally made a play on the name by calling hers "diatoma" after microscopic plants whose cell walls consist of interlocking parts and contain silica (Figure 45).[12] Trinkley's vessels perfectly exploited the aged, encrusted, and deteriorating appearance made possible by *pâte de verre* and introduced the technique to American Studio Glass. Around 1985 she shifted course and transformed the delicate looking, tilted relics into massive, openwork basins made from three grades of frit such as *Spoke* (Figure 46).

Trinkley's classmate at the Rhode Island School of Design, Tina Aufiero, was working with bronze and looking for a way to create specific color and textural effects for her sculpture. She was impressed by the effects that Trinkley was obtaining with her experiments and Aufiero spent 1983 and part of 1984 working with her own version of the technique in a very unlikely place—the Venini factory in Italy. Venini was famous for its blown glass, but for a brief period the company was interested in the possibilities of kilnforming. Artist Laura de Santillana recommended Aufiero's work to her father, Director Ludovico Diaz de Santillana, who invited her to the factory in Murano. There, for the first time, Aufiero had access to an unlimited palette of colored glass. The residency resulted in a series of prototype masks made from dry coarse frits pressed into open molds, however, the pieces did not go into production and Venini discontinued the trials (Figure 48).[13]

During the 1980s, the revival of *pâte de verre* burgeoned internationally. Hobson's initial experience of teaching *pâte de verre* outside of the United Kingdom came in 1987 at the Pilchuck Glass School in Stanwood, Washington. One of her first students was the Japanese artist Keiko Mukaide (Figure 49). Karla Trinkley also had

**Figure: 45**
Karla Trinkley (b. 1956)
United States
*Diatom*, 1984
*Pâte de verre* (pastes of powder and frit)
6" x Diam. 8"

**Figure: 46**
Karla Trinkley (b. 1956)
United States
*Spoke*, 1986
*Pâte de verre* (frits)
12 1/4" x Diam. 14 5/8"
Collection of The Corning Museum of Glass

**Figure: 47**

Tina Aufiero (b. 1959)
United States
Untitled mask of female face,
1980
*Pâte de verre* (dry frit,
ceramic stains,
raw chemicals)
11" x 8" x 4"

**Figure: 48**

Tina Aufiero (b. 1959)
United States; fabricated at
Venini & Co., Murano, Italy
Untitled mask, 1983
*Pâte de verre* (dry frit, ceramic
stains, raw chemicals)
13" x 9" x 3 1/2"

many students from Japan participating in the class that she taught at Pilchuck later the same summer.

*Pâte de verre* later became identified with Japan and the artists there have been key in expanding the limits of the technique. The Tokyo Glass Art Institute, a private school established in 1981 by glass historian Tsuneo Yoshimizu and Keiko Matsuo, was the first institution in Japan to offer instruction in *pâte de verre*. In 1984 the Institute sponsored the *First Japan Pâte de Verre Competition* with 40 students and associates of the school displaying work.[14] The variation of *pâte de verre* favored by the school was the one used by Sotoichi Koshiba—the solid packing of glass powders and frits in a mold—and much of the student work was derivative of historic French styles. An exception was Mihoko Shimoda who was making exquisite, technically sophisticated sake cups and boxes using very fine particles of glass fired to a relatively high temperature giving them unusual translucency. Shimoda's cups are meant to be used; instead of appearing granular and porous, they are solid and highly finished by grinding and polishing (Figure 50). Most impressive was the fact that Shimoda defeated a persistent problem by creating open forms with interior color and patterning as beautiful and controlled as it was on the exterior.

Meanwhile, in 1980 Elizabeth McClure, a graduate of the Edinburgh College of Art, was participating in a research project with the two departments of Materials Science and Art at Sunderland Polytechnic. Her topic was the suitability of various glasses and mold materials for *pâte de verre* and other forms of glass casting. Through Martin Hunt, McClure later met Diana Hobson who shared her research. McClure then traveled to The Corning Museum of Glass to study the ancient uses of glass paste, 19th-century sulphides, and Frederick Carder's kilnforming methods. She also consulted with Jean-Luc Olivié and made her own pilgrimage to the Leperlier brothers who were helpful to her just as they had been to Hobson. Shortly thereafter, while McClure was teaching at the National College of Art and Design in Dublin, she met Tsuneo Yoshimizu who was doing research on glass cutting in Ireland. At his invitation, McClure relocated in 1984 to the Tokyo Glass Art Institute where she taught glassblowing and *pâte de verre*. Perhaps her most important contribution was the encouragement that she gave to her students to break away from the Art Nouveau and Art Moderne styles and to be more inventive. Among McClure's students at the school and at various independent workshops were Keiko Mukaide, Mayumi Shinohara, and Katsuya Ohgita. Ohgita later taught variations of *pâte de verre* to his many students at the Utatsuyama Craft Workshop in Kanazawa.[15] In 1991, Diana Hobson brought her skills to the Miasa Glass Workshop, an innovative program established in 1983 at the Miasa Bunka Center in the mountains of Nagano prefecture. Each year, workshop founder Koji Matano and his colleague Mayumi Shinohara invited two foreign artists to teach. Hobson's class on *pâte de verre*, Miasa's final workshop before permanently closing, brought students in from all over the country.

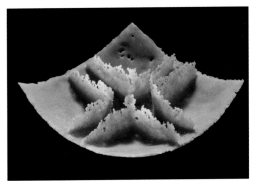 

Today, among the most recognized artists using *pâte de verre* anywhere in the world are husband and wife, Shin-ichi and Kimiake Higuchi. They are relatively new to the glass world and came to it with no formal education in glassmaking. Kimiake, a painter and ceramist, trained also as a professional musician in Italy; Shin-ichi was a practicing industrial designer and architect. Around 1987 they set up a kiln in their garage and began full-time experiments, like so many others, to find a way to combine the characteristics of ceramics and glass. Their research was advanced by studying the *pâte de verre* in the superb collection of Art Nouveau glass at the Kitazawa Museum of Art and in 1988 they exhibited their work for the first time. Since then, their technical advances have been astounding and they have freely shared their knowledge through teaching in workshops worldwide.

The diversity of both Kimiake's and Shin-ichi's styles is as remarkable as their meticulous craftsmanship. The colors they choose are vivid and the imagery bounces from highly realistic to surreal. Most often Kimiake and Shin-ichi draw inspiration from animals, insects, and the fruits, vegetables, and flowers that they grow in their large garden. Both artists occasionally use the human form; Shin-ichi's *Rabbit Tattoo* illustrates his favored technique of forming an intricate mosaic from small *pâte de verre* cut tiles. The parts are fused together to form a patterned sheet, which is heated once more until it "slumps" over a mold, creating a three-dimensional form (Figure 92).

Some of the work by the Higuchis is reminiscent of early French production made in *pâte de verre* and other techniques, but they never use lost wax molds (Figure 89).[16] The high relief and coloration of Kimiake's *Raspberry* vase are very close to the blown vessels with glass powder inclusions and hot worked applications produced by the company of Daum Fréres in Nancy, France, around 1904. Around that time, Daum added *pâte de verre* to its line of blown glass. The production ceased around World War I, but was reactivated in 1968 using designs commissioned from contemporary artists including American Dan Dailey, who has originated eight editions for Daum since 1978 (Figures 51-53). Daum's sculptures are most often made from frit packed in lost wax molds and produced in limited editions of 50 to 200 examples. One of the most well known is Salvador Dalí's draped and dripping clock, *Port-Manteau Montre*, introduced in 1970.

**Figure: 49**
Keiko Mukaide (b. 1954)
Japan
*Kami kana no katachi, No. 1*, 1989
*Pâte de verre* (powder and frit)
2 1/4" x 7 5/8" x 7 5/8"
Collection of
The Corning Museum of Glass

**Figure: 50**
Mihoko Shimoda (b. 1973)
Japan
Sake cups, 1984
*Pâte de verre*
(pastes of powder and frit)
1 1/4" x Diam. 3"
Collection of
The Corning Museum of Glass

The next region where *pâte de verre* took off was the Antipodes. In 1986, Elizabeth McClure traveled from Japan to New Zealand where she ran workshops throughout the country. Native New Zealander Ann Robinson was already fusing crushed glass in lost wax molds and her monumental vessels would eventually build on and update the tradition of Décorchemont from the 1930s. Later that same year McClure began teaching at the Canberra College of Art, Australia, where Klaus Moje headed the Glass Program and was spearheading much of the international enthusiasm for kilnformed glass. It was around this time that Canberra student Etsuko Nishi developed her innovative methods of engineering "ceramic paper" molds and piping glass paste through a pastry bag to make vulnerable looking diatreta-style bowls (Figure 115).

Although some accounts attribute the origins of *pâte de verre* in Asia to mainland China during the Han Dynasty, it appeared in its modern form in Taiwan. In 1987, Hsia-chun (Heinrich) Wang, an actor and film director, moved on his long-standing interest in glass by studying for seven months with Herb Babcock at the College of Art and Design in Detroit, Michigan. After returning to Taiwan and a period of working by himself, Wang joined forces with friends from the film industry, including actress Hui-shan (Loretta) Yang and her husband director Yi Chang, to establish Taiwan's first Studio Glass facility, the New Workshop (Liuli Gongfang). At first the cooperative focused on glassblowing, but soon shifted attention to the production of limited edition *pâte de verre* made in lost wax molds. Yang had encountered *pâte de verre* when her husband purchased several pieces to use as props on a movie set. The process was also compelling because it had ties to ancient Chinese bronze casting. After the inevitable period of struggle and experimentation, the New Workshop held its first exhibition of *pâte de verre* in 1990. Four years later, Heinrich Wang left the New Workshop and with his brother, Yung-shan, founded the Grand Crystal Company, Ltd. (renamed Tittot, Ltd. in 2002) [Figures 139, 140]. Loretta Yang and Yi Chang continued to operate Liuli Gongfang and moved most of its production to Shanghai in 1996 (Figures 145, 146).[17] Both Tittot and Liuli Gongfang have grown into large production operations.

The rise in popularity of *pâte de verre* coincided with a brief, but intense dust-up in the American Studio Glass world during the late 1980s and early 1990s. Because the heretofore definition of Studio Glass had restricted it (more or less) to one-of-a-kind objects, some collectors were shocked to learn that considerable numbers of their purchases (including blown glass) were produced in multiples. They felt that they had been misled into acquiring objects of lesser monetary value—in the same way that a print from an edition is usually priced less than a unique drawing or painting by the same artist. Although multiples are a tradition in glass, ceramics, and other media, it was not supposed to be the case for Studio Glass and even the commercial galleries were not always aware that almost identical works were being made. Because *pâte de verre* and other forms of cast glass are made in molds, they were regarded with the most suspicion. Eventually, when collectors accepted the fact that the unique appearance of cast glass is dependent on the use of molds, and that most Studio Glass editions are small, the flurry died down. In the end, it had the positive effect of encouraging artists and dealers to be more open about the number of pieces made from the same design. Ironically, due to intense lobbying by Steuben Glass on the State legislature, New York exempted glass from the law requiring full disclosure of the numbers produced in each edition.

**Figure: 52**

Dan Dailey (b. 1947)
United States, for
Cristallerie Daum, France
*Le Vent,* 1984,
(from an edition of 150)
*Pâte de verre* (frit; lost wax mold)
13" x 23 1/2" x 4"
Photo: Bill Truslow

In 2005 we are still without an authoritative, uncontested definition of *pâte de verre* and that will probably always be the case. Since the days of Henry Cros, only a fraction of *pâte de verre* has been made in the so-called pure technique of brushing and tamping pastes and slips into open molds. As *Particle Theories* attests, *pâte de verre* is now commonly realized in previously unheard of variations and in combination with other materials. Diana Hobson often included beach sand, small stones, brick dust, bits of metal filings, and screen in her pieces. More recently, Michael Rogers, Head of the Glass Program at the Rochester Institute of Technology, has teamed with Kimiake and Shin-ichi Higuchi for experiments in blowing *pâte de verre* segments picked up on a molten bubble of glass. Mare Saare of Estonia fuses powders directly into sand molds and British artist Christina Kirk has applied *pâte de verre* to ceramic fiber paper to produce "glass paper." Adrianne Evans uses the liquid, gritty glass waste scrounged from the grinding equipment of her fellow artists in Providence, Rhode Island, to build up the layers of her sedimentary glass "rocks." Judy Hill's figures include raku ceramic components and Keith Cummings is well known for his metal incorporations. Markku Salo of Finland sprinkles frit in indentations pressed into a kaolin batting. One of the most recent innovations may be seen in the work of Masayo Odahashi (Figure 118). Like Nicolas Africano (working with Melanie Hunter), Odahashi is one of the few artists following in the steps of Cros by taking advantage of *pâte de verre*'s suitability for the polychrome figure. To form her introspective subjects, Odahashi first casts fine frit in a lost wax mold; after firing and removal from the mold, the figure is painted with high-fire Paradise Paint enamels. At that point, more three-dimensional elements are added and the piece is reinvested and refired. It is such unorthodoxy and innovation, rather than the hair-splitting of terms, which will assure the continued relevancy of *pâte de verre* for contemporary art.

**Figure: 53**

Dan Dailey (b. 1947)
United States, for Cristallerie
Daum, France
*Le Vin,* 1988,
(from an edition of 125)
*Pâte de verre* (frit; lost wax mold)
16 1/2" x 18 1/2" x 8"
Photo: Bill Truslow

## Resources

The Rakow Research Library of The Corning Museum of Glass has compiled extensive bibliographies of historic, modern, and technical *pâte de verre* references including the few listed here. The library may be contacted through the museum's website: www.cmog.org and by e-mail at: Rakow@cmog.org.

## Other recommended materials:

Corning Museum of Glass. *Pâte de verre with Shin-ichi and Kimiake Higuchi, Master Class Series IV*, DVD, The Corning Museum of Glass, Corning, New York, 2001.

Thwaites, Angela. *Mixing with the Best: Investigation and Comparison of Contemporary Working Methods and Mould Making Materials for Use in the Kiln Forming of Glass*, CD-ROM, Royal College of Art, London, 2002.

## Notes

1  Olivié, Jean-Luc, "All of Antiquity in a New Soul," *New Work,* Fall 1987, No. 31, pp. 10-15.
———. "Jalons Pour une Histoire des Pâtes de verre," *Revue de la Céramique et du Verre,* September-October, 1982, No. 6, pp. 8-13.
———. "Henry Cros: Pourquoi et Comment Restituer les Antiques *Pâte de verre?,*" *Annales du 9th Congrès de l'Association Internationale pour l'Histoire du Verre,* L'A.I.H.V. Liege, 1983, pp. 385-399.

2  Fritz Dreisbach, conversation with the author, April 21, 2004.

3  Hobson, Diana. *Pâte de verre: Research into the Techniques,* unpublished manuscript, 1981.

4  Correspondence from Antoine Leperlier to the author, January 22, 2005.

5  Trüjen, Monica and Detlef Tanz. *Verschmelzungen Glas*, Bremen: Stadtwerke Bremen and Galerie Trüjen, 1989.

6  Nkanodo, Kazunobu. "Modern Japanese Glass," *Modern Japanese Glass: Early Meiji to Present,* National Museum of Modern Art, Tokyo, 1982. Special thanks to Yoriko Mizuta of the Hokkaido Museum of Modern Art for her very helpful input and references to Shiro Koshiba's book about his father.

7  Personal correspondence, Frederick Carder archive, Rakow Research Library, The Corning Museum of Glass.

8  Correspondence between Marianne Maderna and the author, July 27, 2004.

9  Argy-Rousseau, Gabriel. *Fabrication de la Pâte de Verre*, undated (probably around 1920), 85 pages of handwritten technical notes. Manuscript purchased in 1961 from Leo Moser. Unedited English translation by Todd Martin.

10  Correspondence between Keith Cummings and the author, January 16, 2005.

11  Leperlier, Antoine and Etienne Leperlier. "Technique de *Pâte de verre*," *Revue de la Céramique et du Verre*, September-October, 1982, No. 6, pp. 14-15.

12  Conversation between Karla Trinkley and the author, January 24, 2005.

13  Correspondence between Tina Aufiero and the author, July 18, 2004-January 30, 2005.

14  Glass Loving Peoples Association and the Tokyo Glass Art Institute. *First Japan Pâte de verre Competition*, Tokyo: 1984.

15  Correspondence between Elizabeth McClure and the author, January 2005.

16  Correspondence between Shin-ichi and Kimiake Higuchi and the author, January 29, 2005.

17  Thanks to both Loretta Yang and Yung-shan Wang for information included in this section of the text.

**Figure 54**
Nicolas Africano (b. 1948)
United States
Untitled (girl sitting on a globe), 2005
with the assistance of Melanie Hunter
*Pâte de verre* (coarse frits; lost wax mold)
16 1/2" x 8" x 14"
Courtesy of Nancy Hoffman Gallery

**Figure: 55**

Margaret Alston (b. 1956)
England
Vessel, 1986
*Pâte de verre* (pastes of powder and fine frit)
4 1/2" x Diam. 3 1/2"
Collection of The Corning Museum of Glass

**Figure: 56**

Margaret Alston (b. 1956)
England
White bowl, 1994
*Pâte de verre* (pastes of powder and fine frit)
5 1/8" x Diam. 5 1/2"
Photo: Ashton James

**Figure: 57**

Margaret Alston (b. 1956)
England
Amethyst bowl, 1999
*Pâte de verre* (pastes of powder and fine frit)
3 1/2" x Diam. 4 3/4"
Photo: Kate Gadsby

**Figure: 58**

Doug Anderson (b. 1952)
United States
Acorn bowl, 1982
*Pâte de verre* (pastes of powder and fine frit;
lost wax mold)
5" x Diam. 8 1/2"
Collection of Patricia and Paul Stankard

**Figure: 59 (with detail)**

Doug Anderson (b. 1952)
United States
*Finders Creepers,* 1986
*Pâte de verre* (pastes of powder and fine frit; lost wax mold,
individual elements molded from life)
3 3/4" x 29 1/2" x 14 1/2"
The First Rakow Commission
Collection of The Corning Museum of Glass

**Figure: 60**

Tina Aufiero (b. 1959)
United States
*la donna qui dorme sopra gli alberi, tutti des alberi sonna soi*
(the woman who sleeps in the trees, all the dreams belong to her),
5 parts, 1986
*Pâte de verre* (dry powders and frit, raw chemicals; lost wax molds)
Each: 11"-12" x 9"-12" x 3 1/2"-5"

**Figure: 61**

Pat Bako (b. 1975)
United States
*Carnivale*, 2003
*Pâte de verre* (pastes of powder and fine frit)
9" x 11" x 6"
Photo: Dan Neuberger

**Figure: 62**

Anna Boothe (b. 1958)
United States
*Fish or Cut Bait,* 1991
*Pâte de verre* (fused highway beads,
lost wax mold); mixed-media
23" x 13 1/2" x 4"
Photo: Eric Mitchell

**Figure: 63**

Anna Boothe (b. 1958)
United States
*Spring Off,* 1996
*Pâte de verre* (frit and
copper carbonate powder,
lost wax mold); wood
45" x 30" x 8"
Photo: Eric Mitchell

**Figure: 64**

Anna Boothe (b. 1958)
United States
*Lightning Dancers,* 2001
*Pâte de verre* (frit in multiple molds)
28" x 18" x 11 1/2"
Photo: Bruce Miller

**Figure: 65 (with detail)**

Charissa Brock (b. 1971)
United States
*Springtime Dance,* 2004
*"Patisserie de verre"* (wafers of dry frit fused without a mold);
black bamboo, waxed linen thread, steel
34 1/2" x 14" x 14"
Photo: Dan Kavitka

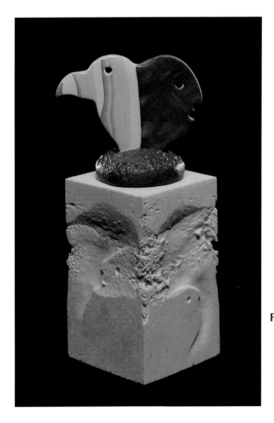

**Figure: 66**

Keith Brocklehurst (b. 1946)
England
*Spirit Box,* 1985
*Pâte de verre* (powder and frit)
6" x 2 1/2" x 2 1/2"
Collection of The Corning Museum of Glass

**Figure: 67**

Tessa Clegg (b. 1946)
England
Bowl, 1983
*Pâte de verre* (frit, lost wax mold)
2 1/2" x Diam. 6 3/4"
Collection of The Corning Museum of Glass

**Figure: 68**

Tessa Clegg (b. 1946)
England
*Vertex II,* 2004-2005
*Pâte de verre* (base: billets melted into
lost wax mold; insert: frit)
3" x 11" x 7 1/2"
Photo: Peter Abrahams

**Figure: 69**

Ros Conway (b. 1951)
England
*Blue Nereid,* 1997
(from an edition of 3)
*Pâte de verre* (pastes of
powder and fine lead frit)
8 1/4" x 4 1/4"

**Figure: 70**

Ros Conway (b. 1951)
England
*Red Spiral,* 2001
*Pâte de verre* (pastes of
powder and lead frit)
3 1/8" x 7 1/2" x 6 1/4"

**Figure: 71**

Ros Conway (b. 1951)
England
*Green Steps,* 2001
*Pâte de verre* (pastes of
powder and lead frit)
4 3/4" x 8 1/4" x 6 1/4"

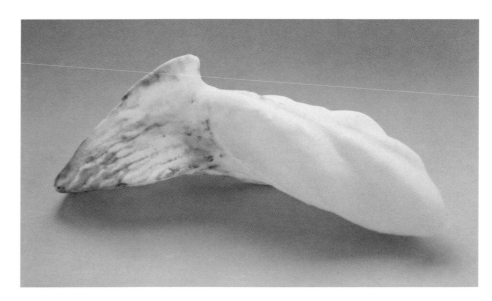

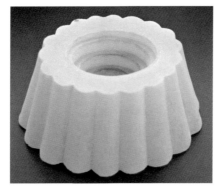 

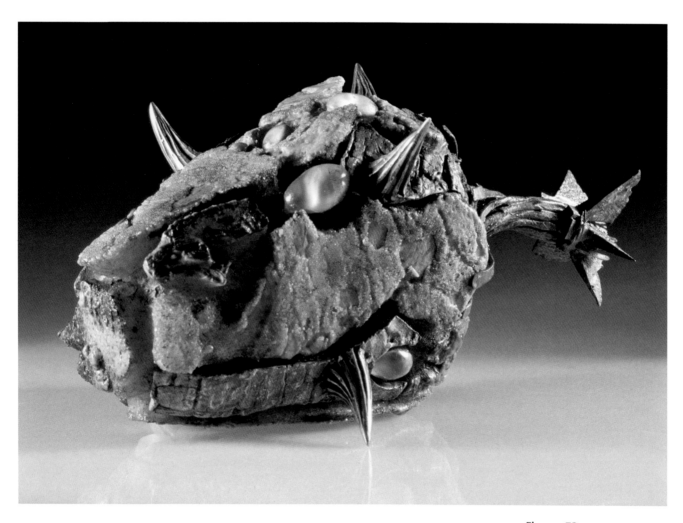

**Figure: 72**

Keith Cummings (b. 1940)
England
*Fusil,* 2000
*Pâte de verre* (frit with precast
surface sections); cast bronze
5 1/2" x 9" x 4 3/4"

**Figure: 73**

Dan Dailey (b. 1947)
United States
*Circus Surrealists* from the *Circus Vase* series, 2000
Blown and acid-polished glass, *pâte de verre* and
flameworked details; gold-plated bronze
19" x 14" x 14"
Photo: Anthony Gomez
Courtesy of Leo Kaplan Modern

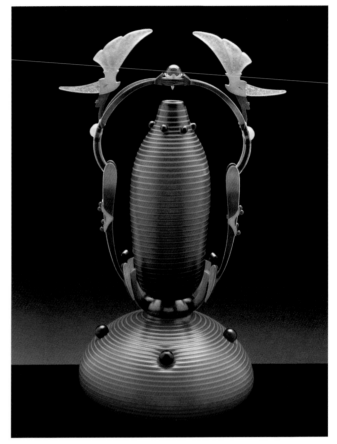

**Figure: 74**

Dan Dailey (b. 1947)
United States
*Masquerade* from the *Circus Vase* series, 2002
Blown and acid-polished glass, *pâte de verre* and
flameworked details; copper and gold-plated bronze
22" x 15 1/2" x 11"
Photo: Bill Truslow
Courtesy of Imago Galleries

**Figure: 75**

    Stephen Paul Day (b. 1954)
    United States
    *Fetish Object,* 1998
    *Pâte de verre* (lead frit, masonry stains;
    lost wax mold)
    6 1/4" x 10 1/2" x 9 1/4"
    Collection of the Museum of American Glass,
    Wheaton Village

**Figure: 76**

    Stephen Paul Day (b. 1954)
    United States
    *Chief Seattle's Hand,* 1998
    *Pâte de verre* (lead frit, masonry stains;
    lost wax mold)
    11" x 7 3/4" x 8"
    Collection of the Museum of American Glass,
    Wheaton Village

**Figure: 77**

Steven Easton (b. 1961)
United States
*The Snow Queen's Realm*, 108 to 324 parts, 2004-2005
*Pâte de verre* (powder and frit, lost wax molds)
Overall dimensions vary, each part: 1" x Diam. 1/2"-6 1/2" x Diam. 6"

**Figure: 78**

Adrianne Evans (b. 1972)
United States
*Sediment,* 2002
*Pâte de verre* (fused glass sediment
collected from the studios of
various artists)
16" x 22" x 16"

**Figure: 79**

Adrianne Evans (b. 1972)
United States
*Four Rocks,* 2002-2004
Two rocks: *pâte de verre* (fused glass
sediment collected from the studios
of various artists)
Two rocks: stacked autumn and
spring tree leaves
Each group of two: 2" x 5" x 3"

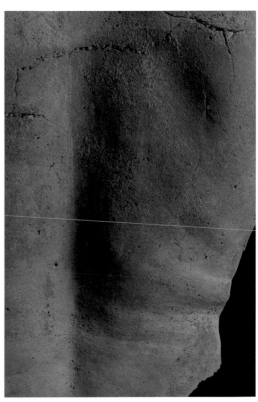

**Figure: 80 (with details)**

Adrianne Evans (b. 1972)
United States
*Our II*, 2004
*Pâte de verre*
(frit; mold cast from life)
Overall: 22" x 40" x 5"

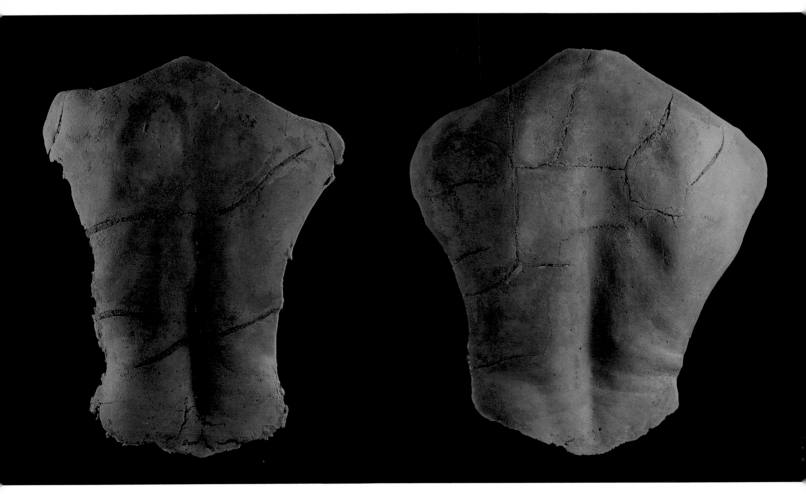

**Figure: 81**

Penny Fuller (b. 1969)
Australia
Two *Leaf Vessels* from the *Autumn Series*, 2004
*Pâte de verre* (pastes of frit)
Orange Leaf: 1 3/4" x 7 3/4" x 4 3/4"
Yellow Leaf: 2" x 8" x 4 1/2"
Photo: G. Hancock

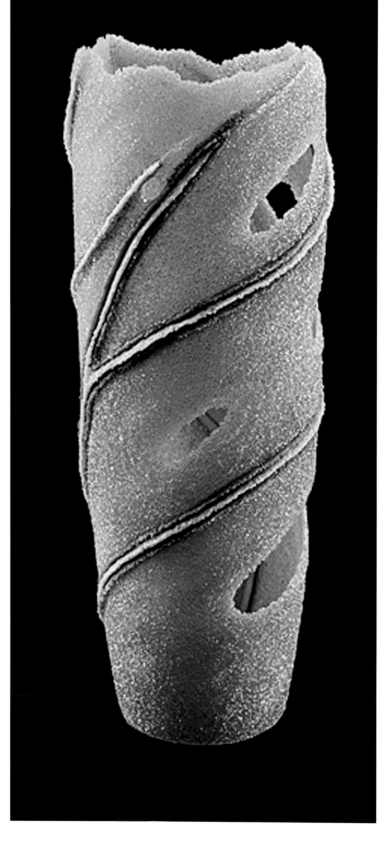

**Figure: 82**

Penny Fuller (b. 1969)
Australia
*Palm Leaf Vessel* (cylindrical), 2005
*Pâte de verre* (pastes of frit)
10" x Diam. 3 3/4"
Photo: G. Hancock

**Figure: 83**

Robin Grebe (b. 1957)
United States
*Historical Analogy,* 1986
*Pâte de verre* (powders and frit)
13 1/4" x 4 3/8" x 2 3/4"
Collection of The Corning Museum of Glass

**Figure: 84**

Robin Grebe (b. 1957)
United States
Triptych, 1989
*Pâte de verre* (powders and frit); mixed media
33 1/2" x 7 1/4" x 3"
Collection of Patricia and Paul Stankard

**Figure: 85**

Marie Aimée Grimaldi (b. 1958, Algeria)
France
*YZ*, 1992
*Pâte de verre* (powders and frit,
lost wax molds)
5 1/4" x 11 1/4" x 8"
Courtesy of Barry Friedman, Ltd.

**Figure: 86**

Marie Aimée Grimaldi
(b. 1958, Algeria)
France
*www.dante.hell*, 2000
*Pâte de verre* (powders and frit,
lost wax molds
8" x 8 1/4" x 9 3/4"
Courtesy of Barry Friedman, Ltd.

**Figure: 87**

Marie Aimée Grimaldi
(b. 1958, Algeria)
France
*52nd Street, 3 Bloc Latter* [sic], 2000
*Pâte de verre* (powders and frit,
lost wax molds)
8 5/8" x 8 1/8" x 10 1/4"
Courtesy of Barry Friedman, Ltd.

**Figure: 88**

Page Hazlegrove (1956–1997)
United States
*Interior with Vessels,* 1993
*Pâte de verre* (powder and frit)
25 1/4" x 14" x 5"
Gift of Mike and Annie Belkin
Collection of
The Corning Museum of Glass

**Figure: 89**

Kimiake Higuchi
(b. 1948)
Japan
*Raspberry* Vase, 2001
*Pâte de verre* (pastes of powders and frit; details molded from life)
19" x Diam. 12 1/2"

**Figure: 90**

Kimiake Higuchi (b. 1948)
Japan
*Rabbit*, 1992
*Pâte de verre* (pastes of powders and frit;
details molded from life); glass eyes and
teeth, hammered copper
6 3/4" x 19 3/4" 10 1/2"

**Figure: 91**
Shin-ichi Higuchi (b. 1947)
Japan
*Beehive*, 1994
*Pâte de verre* (powders and frit;
fused and slumped mosaic)
5 1/2" x Diam. 15 3/4"

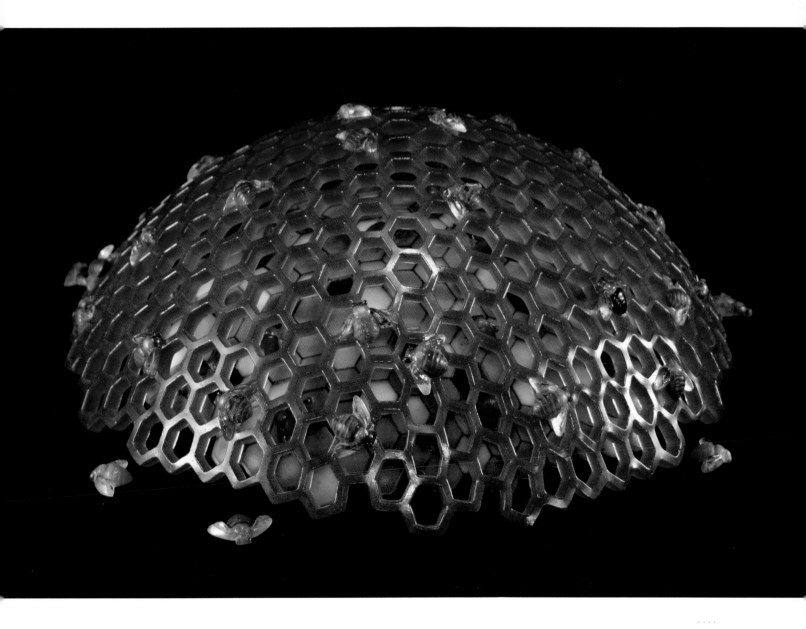

**Figure 92**

Shin-ichi Higuchi (b. 1947)
Japan
*Rabbit Tattoo,* 2002
*Pâte de verre* (powders and frit;
fused and slumped mosaic)
26 1/2" x 15" x 5 1/8"
Courtesy of Habatat Galleries

**Figure: 93**

Judy Hill (b. 1953)
United States
*Little World,* 1989-1990
*Pâte de verre* (coarse frit; lost wax molds);
glazed and raku-fired ceramic
9" x 3 1/2"
Collection of Patricia and Paul Stankard

**Figure: 94**

Judy Hill (b. 1953)
United States
*Jump,* 1993
*Pâte de verre* (coarse frit; lost wax molds);
glazed and raku-fired ceramic
20" x 11" x 5 1/4"
Collection of The Corning Museum of Glass

**Figure: 95**

Judy Hill (b. 1953)
United States
*Walk in the Park*, 2004-2005
Pâte de verre (coarse frit; lost wax molds);
glazed and raku-fired ceramic
17" x 12" x 7"

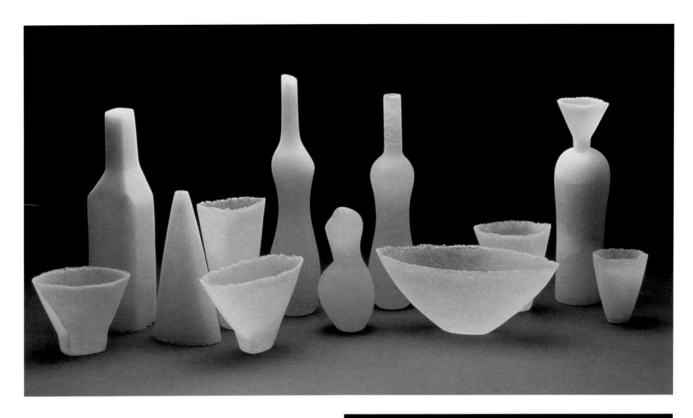

**Figure: 96**

Deborah Horrell (b. 1953)
United States
*Still Life – Lineage of White,* 12 parts, 2002
*Pâte de verre* (frit); carved alabaster
Overall: 13 1/8" x 36" x 8"
Courtesy of Elizabeth Leach Gallery
Photo: Paul Foster

**Figure: 97**

Deborah Horrell (b. 1953)
United States
*Struck by Lightning,* 2 parts, 2003
*Pâte de verre* (frit)
Overall: 15" x 9 1/2" x 4 1/2"
Courtesy of Elizabeth Leach Gallery
Photo: Paul Foster

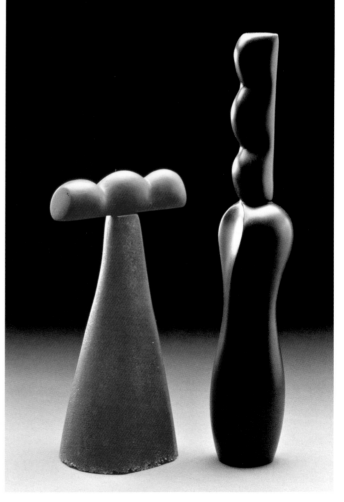

**Figure: 98**

Ursula Huth (b. 1952)
Germany

*Cargoes-matcho gonda,*
4 parts, 1995/1997

*Pâte de verre* (powders
and frit; lost wax and
clay molds); engraved,
cast metal net
(lost wax mold)

10 1/4" x 12 1/2" x 7 1/2"
Photo: Claus Iden

**Figure: 99**

Anja Isphording (b. 1964)
Germany
*# 83, 2003*
*Pâte de verre* (frit; lost wax mold)
8 3/4" x Diam. 8 1/4"
Courtesy of Heller Gallery
Photo: Ken Mayer

**Figure: 100**

Anja Isphording (b. 1964)
Germany
*# 80, 2003*
*Pâte de verre* (frit; lost wax mold)
9 1/2" x Diam. 7"
Courtesy of
Bullseye Connection Gallery
Photo: Ken Mayer

**Figure: 101**

Kinuko Ito (b. 1942)
Japan
*Night Cap*, set of 6 cups, 1984
*Pâte de verre* (powders and frit)
Each: 2 1/2" x 2 3/4"
Collection of The Corning Museum of Glass

**Figure: 102**
    Päivi Kekäläinen (b. 1961)
    Finland
    *Idullaan (Germination),* 2002
    *Pâte de verre* (frit, precast surface
    sections); wire ties
    3 3/4″ x 8″ x 8″

**Figure: 103**
    Päivi Kekäläinen (b. 1961)
    Finland
    *Mätäs (Tussock),* 2002
    *Pâte de verre* (frit); wire ties
    3 1/2″ x 8″ x 8″

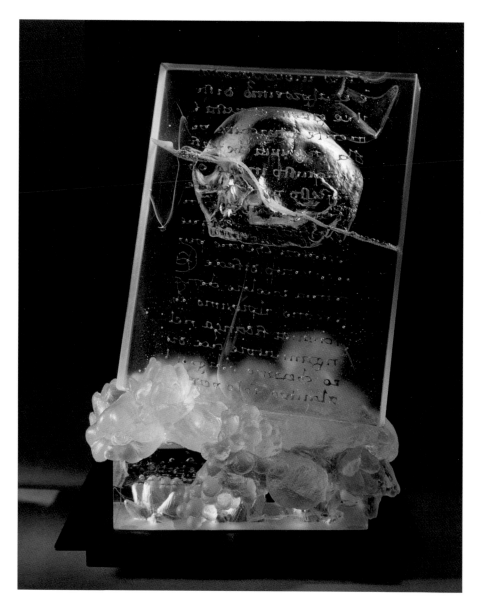

**Figure: 104**

Antoine Leperlier (b. 1953)
France
*Ombre Portée VII (Cast Shadow VII)*,
with internal anamorphic skull cavity,
2000
Melted optical billets (engraved letters
filled with powder; lost wax molds)
metal base
27 1/2" x 17" x 12 1/2"
Courtesy of Habatat Galleries
Photo: Jalain

**Figure: 105**

Antoine Leperlier (b. 1953)
France
*Coupe Vanité X*, 2004
*Pâte de verre* (frit and powder;
lost wax molds)
8" x 8 3/4" x 4 3/4"
Courtesy of Habatat Galleries

**Figure: 106**

Alicia Lomné (b. 1972, Corsica)
United States
*Joining,* 2004
*Pâte de verre* (pastes of powder and frit)
12 5/8" x 7 7/8" x 5 1/4"

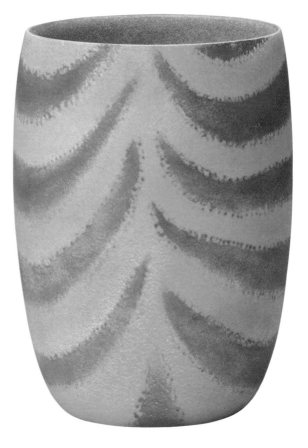

**Figure: 107**

Alicia Lomné (b. 1972, Corsica)
United States
*Tiger Moth Vessel,* 2005
*Pâte de verre* (pastes of powders and frit)
10 1/4" x 7 1/4" x 5 1/2"

**Figure: 108**

Alicia Lomné
(b. 1972, Corsica)
United States
*Slumber II,* 2005
*Pâte de verre* (pastes of
powder and frit)
35" x 9 1/4" x 7 1/2"

Alicia Lomné
(b. 1972, Corsica)
United States
*Slumber III,* 2005
*Pâte de verre* (pastes of
powder and frit)
35" x 9 1/4" x 7 1/2"

**Figure: 109**

Linda MacNeil (b. 1954)
United States
*Mesh 59-97* from the *Mesh Necklace* series, 1997
*Pâte de verre;* acid polished, 24k gold-plated brass
Pendant: H. 4"
Photo: Bill Truslow

**Figure: 110**

Linda MacNeil (b. 1954)
United States
*Egyptian Reed 36-03* from the *Floral Necklace* series, 2003
*Pâte de verre* (green); acid-polished, amber glass,
24k gold-plated brass
Pendant: H. 3 1/4"
Photo: Bill Truslow

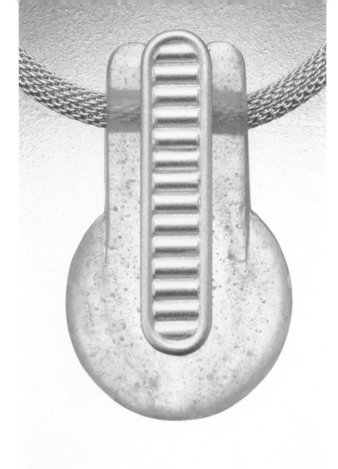

**Figure: 111**

Linda MacNeil (b. 1954)
United States
*Ruby Bliss 56-04* from the *Floral Necklace* series, 2004
*Pâte de verre* (aqua); acid-polished, red glass,
black and cream Vitrolite, polished; 24k gold-plated brass
Pendant: 2 1/2" x 1 1/4" x 5/8"
Photo: Bill Truslow

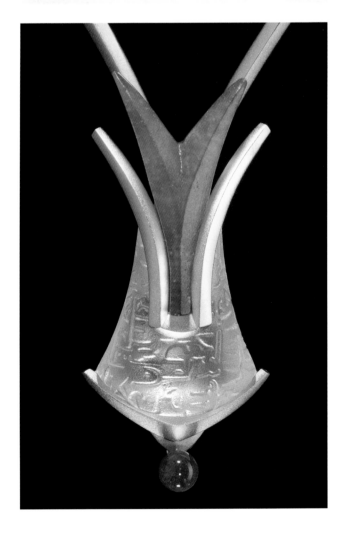

**Figure: 112**

Hilton McConnico (b. 1943)
United States, for Cristallerie Daum, France
*Nevada Bowl* from the *Cactus* series, 1987
(from an edition of 950)
*Pâte de verre* (base: powder and frit;
lost wax mold), blown glass bowl
7" x Diam. 12 1/4"
Collection of The Corning Museum of Glass

**Figure: 113**

Michael McDonough (b. 1951)
Executed by Tina Aufiero
United States
*Child's Chair,* 1991
*Pâte de verre* (powder and frit, four lost wax molds)
26 1/4" x 12 1/4" x 12 3/4"
Gift of Michael McDonough in honor of
Metropolis Magazine's "Design Explorations"
Collection of The Corning Museum of Glass

**Figure: 114**

Catharine Newell (b. 1947)
United States
*Unicyclist* triptych, 2005
Fused powder and frit drawing on kilnformed sheet glass
Each panel: 30" x 6" x 7/8"
Photo: Paul Foster

**Figure: 115**

Etsuko Nishi (b. 1955)
Japan
*Lace Cage,* 1990
*Pâte de verre* (pastes of powder and frit;
ceramic fiber paper mold)
6 1/8" x Diam. 9 3/4"
Collection of The Corning Museum of Glass

**Figure: 116**

Etsuko Nishi (b. 1955)
Japan
*Layered Vessel #1 (Cherry Blossom),* 2004
*Pâte de verre* (frit; ceramic fiber paper mold)
11 3/4" x 15 3/4"
Courtesy of Marx-Saunders Gallery

**Figure: 117**

Etsuko Nishi (b. 1955)
Japan
*Layered Vessel #10 (Flower Basket),* 2004
*Pâte de verre* (frit; ceramic fiber paper mold)
14 1/8" x 18 7/8" x 11 3/4"
Courtesy of Marx-Saunders Gallery

**Figure: 118**

Masayo Odahashi (b. 1975)
Japan
*Calm of Water III,* 2004
*Pâte de verre* (frit, enamels; lost wax mold)
20" x 6 3/4" x 7"

Masayo Odahashi (b. 1975)
Japan
*Calm of Water VI,* 2004
*Pâte de verre* (frit, enamels; lost wax mold)
20" x 6 3/4" x 7"

**Figure: 119**

Momoo Omuro (b. 1969)
Japan
Bowls, 2004
*Pâte de verre* (pastes of powders and frit)
Tallest: 4 3/4" x Diam. 8 3/4"

**Figure: 120**

Momoo Omuro (b. 1969)
Japan
Bowl, 2004
*Pâte de verre* (pastes of powders and frit)
4 3/4" x Diam. 8 3/4"

**Figure: 121**

Gaetano Pesce (b. 1939)
Italy; fabricated at le Centre International de
Recherche sur le Verre et les Arts Plastique (CIRVA),
Marseilles, France
*Réussite 2*, 1988-1992
*Pâte de verre*
8" x 13" x 9 1/2"
Collection of The Corning Museum of Glass

**Figure: 122**

Sibylle Peretti (b. 1964)
Germany
*Boy Holding Bird,* 1997
*Pâte de verre* (frits;
lost wax mold)
18 1/2" x 5 1/2" x 3 1/2"
Collection of the
Museum of American Glass,
Wheaton Village

**Figure: 123**

Seth Randal (b. 1957)
United States
*Les Moutons Onceés,* 1992
*Pâte de verre*
13" x Diam. 16"
Collection of the
Museum of American Glass,
Wheaton Village

**Figure: 124**

Gerhard Ribka (b. 1955)
Germany
*Das Boot im Schlaf
(The Boat Asleep),* 2004
*Pâte de verre* (powder and
frit); wood, plaster,
pencil, pigment
Frame: 4" x 4" x 2"

**Figure: 125**

Gerhard Ribka (b. 1955)
Germany
*Warten (Waiting),* 2004
*Pâte de verre* (powder and
frit); silver stain, brass leaf,
wood, plaster, paper,
pencil, crayon
Frame: 6 1/4" x 8 1/8" x 2"

**Figure 126**

Gerhard Ribka (b. 1955)
Germany
*Das goldene Zimmer (The Golden Room)*, 2004
*Pâte de verre* (powder and frit); silver stain, wood,
plaster, gift wrapping paper, pencil
Frame: 5 1/2" x 5 1/2" x 2"

Gerhard Ribka (b. 1955)
Germany
*Heimkehr, verblichen (Homecoming, Faded)*, 2004
*Pâte de verre* (powder and frit); refractory material,
wood, plaster, pigment
Frame: 6 1/4" x 6 3/4" x 2"

Gerhard Ribka (b. 1955)
Germany
*Tauben und Flugzeug (Pigeons and Airplane)*, 2004
*Pâte de verre* (powder and frit); refractory material,
pigment
Tallest: 2" x 1 1/2" x 1 3/4"

**Figure: 127**

Gerhard Ribka (b. 1955)
Germany
*Knospe (Bud)*, 2004
*Pâte de verre* (powder and frit); silver stain,
glass button, brass wire
1 3/8" x 4 3/4" x 4"

**Figure: 128**

Victoria Rodgers (b. 1950)
New Zealand
*Fire Vases* from the *Dancing in the South Pacific* series, 2003
*Pâte de verre* (hot-formed stringers [glass threads], pastes of frit)
Each: 11" x Diam. 2 1/4"

**Figure: 129**

Victoria Rodgers (b. 1950)
New Zealand
*Earth Vase* from the *Dancing in the South Pacific* series, 2003
*Pâte de verre* (hot-formed stringers [glass threads], pastes of frit)
11" x Diam. 2 1/4"

**Figure: 130**

Mare Saare (b. 1955)
Estonia
*Desert I: Khomsa*, 2002
*Pâte de verre*
(brushed slips of powder)
9 1/2" x 9 1/2"

**Figure: 131**

Mare Saare (b. 1955)
Estonia
*Desert 2: Night,* 2002
*Pâte de verre*
(brushed slips of powder)
9" x 9"

**Figure: 132**

Markku Salo (b. 1954)
Finland
*Torso,* 2003
*Pâte de verre* (frit;
kaolin batting mold)
47 1/4" x 98 1/2"

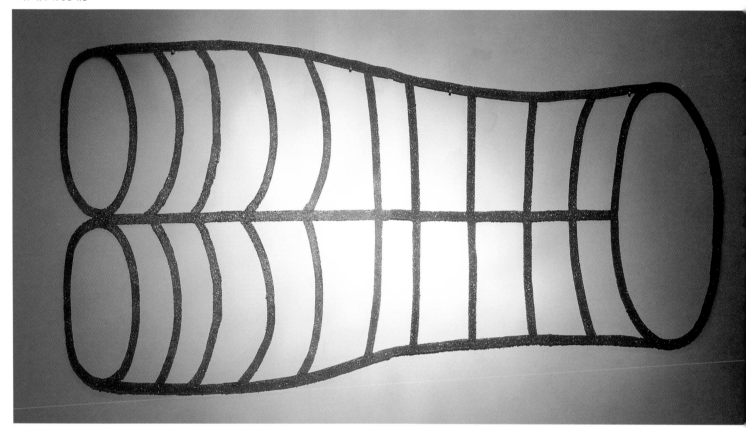

**Figure: 133**

Woo-Mee Suh (b. 1958)
Korea
Untitled figure, 1992
*Pâte de verre*
15" x 6" x 8"
Collection of the
Museum of American Glass,
Wheaton Village

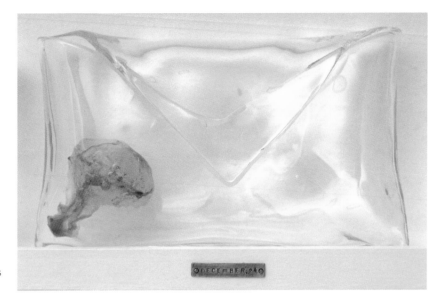

**Figure: 134 (with detail)**
Erika Tada (b. 1975)
Japan
*Letter,* 2004, 30 parts
Blown glass envelopes with *pâte de verre* inserts
Overall dimensions vary: 40" x 59" x 4"

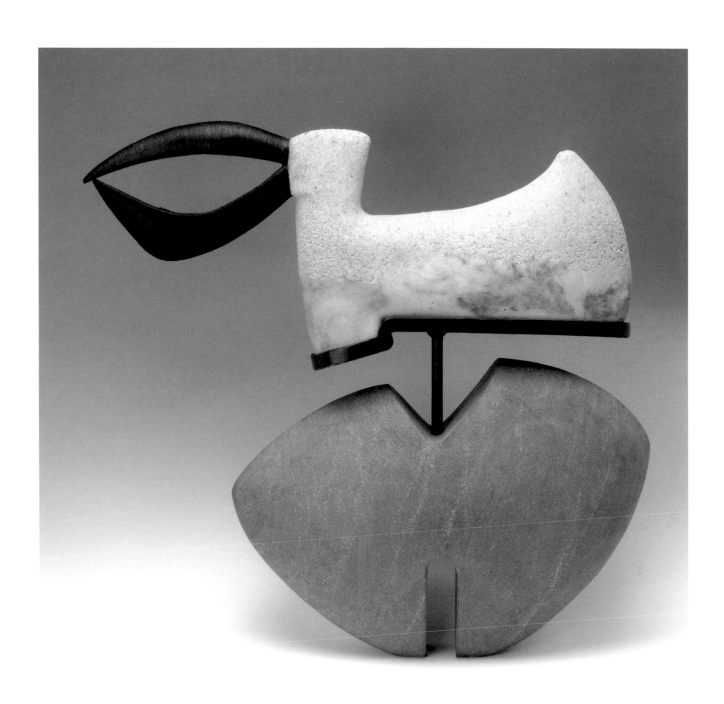

**Figure: 135**

Karla Trinkley (b. 1956)
United States
*Winged Bird,* 2004
*Pâte de verre* (pastes of powder and frit);
carved wood, granite
32" x 30" x 7"

**Figure: 136**

Sylvie Vandenhoucke (b. 1969)
Belgium
Untitled Vessel, 1999
*Pâte de verre* (pastes of powder and frit);
black patinated copper wire
H. 4"

**Figure: 137**

Sylvie Vandenhoucke (b. 1969)
Belgium
Untitled Vessel, 2000
*Pâte de verre* (pastes of powder and frit); silver wire
H. 6"

**Figure: 138**

Sylvie Vandenhoucke (b. 1969)
Belgium
*Raw Target,* 2004, multiple parts
*Pâte de verre* (frit and oxides)
Diam. 69"-79"

**Figure: 139**

Heinrich (Hsia-chun) Wang, (b. 1953, Indonesia)
Taiwan, for Tittot, Ltd., Taiwan (fabricated in
Shanghai, China)
*Cloud Threading the Daylight* from the *Landscape
and Wind* series, 2004 (from an edition of 6)
*Pâte de verre* (frits; lost wax mold)
28" x 23 1/2" x 13 3/4"
Courtesy of Tittot, Ltd.

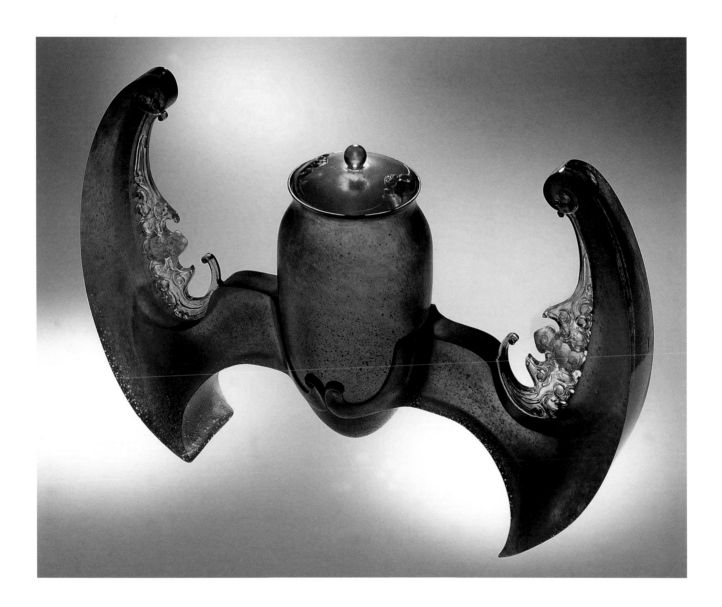

**Figure: 140**

Heinrich (Hsia-chun) Wang,
(b. 1953, Indonesia)
Taiwan, for Tittot, Ltd., Taiwan
(fabricated in Shanghai, China)
*Soaring Happiness* from the
*Heroes* series, 2004
(from an edition of 43)
*Pâte de verre* (powders and frits;
lost wax mold)
11 3/4" x 19" x 3"
Courtesy of Tittot, Ltd.

**Figure: 141**

James Watkins (b. 1955)
United States
*Two Leaves,* 1997
*Pâte de verre* (lead frit,
lost wax molds); bronze,
wood
8" x 44" x 5 1/4"

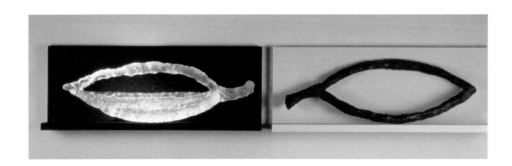

**Figure: 142**

James Watkins (b. 1955)
United States
*BOE (Bird on Edge),* 1999
*Pâte de verre* (lead frit,
lost wax mold)
15" x 9" x 5"

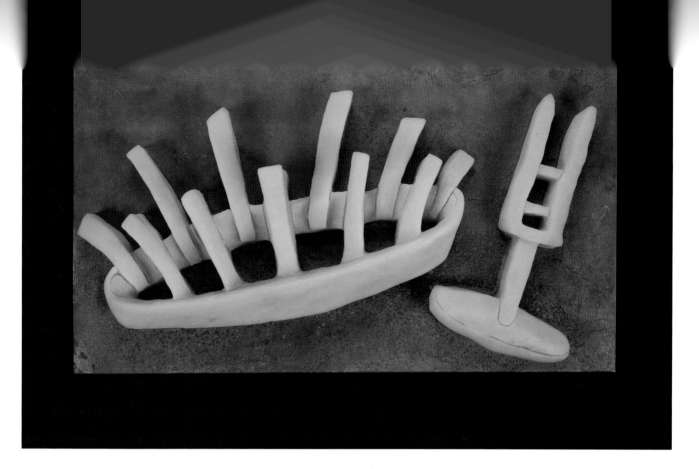

**Figure: 143**

Jack Wax (b. 1954)
United States
*Circus Lights,* 1986
*Pâte de verre* (powder and frit); steel mount
13" x 23 3/4"
Collection of The Corning Museum of Glass

**Figure: 144**

Emma Wood (b. 1969)
England
Vase, 1999
*Pâte de verre* (pastes of powders and frit)
7 1/2"
Gift of Barry Friedman, Ltd., New York
Collection of the Chrysler Museum of Art, Norfolk, VA

**Figure: 145**

Loretta (Hui-shan) Yang (b. 1952)
Taiwan; for Liuli Gongfang Crystal Co., Ltd.,
Shanghai, China
*The One and Only,* 2004 (from an edition of 12)
*Pâte de verre* (powders and frit; lost wax mold);
cast molten glass
10 5/8" x Diam. 23 1/2"
Courtesy of Liuli Gongfang Crystal Co., Ltd.

**Figure: 146**

Loretta (Hui-shan) Yang (b. 1956)
Taiwan, for Liuli Gongfang Crystal Co., Ltd., Shanghai, China
*The Other Side of Water,* 2004 (from an edition of 16)
*Pâte de verre* (powders and frit; lost wax mold);
cast molten glass, engraved
9 1/2" x Diam. 23 1/2"
Courtesy of Liuli Gongfang Crystal Co., Ltd.

Wheaton Village
1501 Glasstown Road
Millville, New Jersey 08332-1566 USA

TEL:  (856) 825-6800
FAX:  (856) 825-2410
WEB: www.wheatonvillage.org

The Museum of American Glass is a core component of Wheaton Village in Millville, New Jersey, a 501(c)(3), nonprofit organization. The Museum houses the most comprehensive collection of American glass in the country, and is fully accredited by the American Association of Museums.